THE FIVE
OFFICES FOR TODAY

Book 1 – The Fivefold Office Series

COLETTE TOACH

AMI BOOKSHOP

www.ami-bookshop.com

The Fivefold Offices for Today
Book 1 – The Fivefold Office Series

ISBN-10: 1-62664-115-3
ISBN-13: 978-1-62664-115-0

1st Printing June 2016

Published by **Apostolic Movement International, LLC**
E-mail Address: admin@ami-bookshop.com
Web Address: www.ami-bookshop.com

Contents

THE FIVEFOLD MINISTRY FOUNDATION

Chapter 01 – The Fivefold Ministry Foundation

I could not possibly live without all the fingers on my hand. Now, I suppose that I could do a lot with my thumb, but if my thumb was all I had, there would be some things that I could not do.

I could not pick my nose with my thumb because that would be uncomfortable. (Nasty image, but I am sure it conveys my point!) That is how it is in the ministry. Fortunately for us, the Scriptures clearly lay out what the functions are.

As there are five fingers on my hand, so has the Lord set five ministry leaders in the church that help assist the rest of the body. Yet, it seems that the church has been complacent.

We feel that we do not really need the thumb and the forefinger. We think we can just get by with three fingers. Have you ever sprained a finger or cut it in an awkward spot? When you have done this, something as simple as trying to button a shirt becomes a whole thing.

We wonder why the body of Christ is in the disarray that it is. We wonder why there are so many different doctrines and why there is so much conflict. It is because there is no balance.

If we do not have all the fingers on our hand, how can we take care of the rest of the body? Having a shower and getting dressed with missing fingers is difficult!

In this book, I am going to talk about the hand - the fivefold ministry. This is an extensive subject that we have done a lot of teaching on, but, if you want a bit of an understanding, you can read the whole book of Ephesians.

There Paul lays down some gospel truths that we seem to have forgotten in this day and age.

Now when I say the term – fivefold ministry, a lot of things come to mind. For many believers, a blank comes to mind. They think, "What is the fivefold ministry?"

By the end of this chapter, you will not only know what the fivefold ministry is, but you will know what part each of them is meant to be playing in the church. Finally, as we look at all these things, perhaps you will be able to identify your part, if God has called you to one of these offices.

Not for Everyone

Before I get too far into this chapter, I want to clarify that this calling is not for every believer. These are five leadership offices in the Church. I have done other teachings on body ministries as well because there are many different ministries given to the body of Christ. However, you would not think so if you spoke to a prophet. (You can find these teachings in the *Called to the Ministry* book)

As far as some prophets are concerned, the only fivefold ministry is the prophetic ministry. So, it depends on which camp you are coming from. However, there is more than the fivefold ministry.

There are other ministries and functions, but we are not going to get into that right now. I am just going to speak about the fivefold ministry specifically.

When we start looking at the book of Ephesians, we start seeing something interesting.

Paul begins by speaking to the Gentiles and saying, "Do you know that you are a part of the body – fellow citizens in the house of God?"

> *Ephesians 2:19 Now therefore you are no longer strangers and foreigners, but fellow citizens with the saints, and of the household of God*

Paul Uncovers the Mystery

Paul says to the Gentiles, "You are part of this body. God has picked you out and chosen you to be where you are right now. You have a specific place in the body." Then, he goes from there in Ephesians 3:3 and says, "Do you know that there is a mystery?"

The mystery was that no one knew up until the New Testament that the Gentiles would be part of the promise. As far as the Jews were concerned, the Savior would only come to the Jews. The disciples did not even know until the very end how the sacrifice of Christ would change everything.

I daresay that the disciples did not get it until Peter stood in front of the Gentiles and the Holy Spirit came on them. I can imagine that everybody stood there thinking, "What just happened?"

In the book of Ephesians, Paul shows us a full picture of the body that included a mystery - a new revelation that Gentiles would be grafted into this vine and be part of this body as well.

One Body

Then he goes further, in Ephesians 4, and starts laying things down.

Ephesians 4:4-7 says,

> *There is one body and one Spirit, just as you were called in one hope of your calling;*
> *5 one Lord, one faith, one baptism;*
> *6 one God and Father of all, who is above all, and through all, and in you[a] all.*
> *7 But to each one of us grace was given according to the measure of Christ's gift.*

He speaks about Christians as a whole here. He says that there is one body. He has taken three whole chapters of Ephesians to explain that you are a part of the body. You have the picture of the body by now.

After this he is saying that not only are you a part of the body, but you have a calling within this body. Then, before he gets into the callings, he emphasizes that there is one Lord, one faith, one baptism, one God and Father of all who is above all, through all and in you all. (Eph 4:5)

He is basically saying, "God is in you. You are in God. There is one body. There is a place for you in the body." Perhaps, the Ephesians were a bit slow because Paul felt the need to repeat himself a whole lot.

Then, we get onto the next part. Here Paul is building up and showing that there is even more. He is building this plot up nicely. He would have done so well in Hollywood!

Origination of the Term "Fivefold Ministry"

In Ephesians 4 verses 11-13 he says,

> *And He Himself gave some to be apostles, some prophets, some evangelists, and some pastors and teachers,*
> *12 for the equipping of the saints for the work of ministry, for the edifying of the body of Christ,*
> *13 till we all come to the unity of the faith and of the knowledge of the Son of God, to a perfect man, to the measure of the stature of the fullness of Christ*

Now, if you heard the term "fivefold ministry" and you do not know what it is, here is the scripture that shows where it originates. It does not specifically say the words "fivefold ministry", but it is much easier to say "fivefold ministry" than, "The Lord has called apostles, prophets, teachers, pastors and evangelists in this day and age...!"

I love verse twelve and thirteen where he breaks it down and shows that these are some very important callings here. He says that all of the fivefold are meant to mature and equip believers. They are meant to bring them to unanimous agreement concerning the faith, to bring them to the knowledge of the Son of God, and to bring them to a mature man and the level of maturity of the complete Christ.

He is telling us that the fivefold ministry is meant to be accomplishing this right now. The difference lies in how each of the fivefold ministry accomplishes this function. This is where your calling lies today.

The Fivefold Ministry Function

Every one of the fivefold ministry is meant to be fulfilling verses twelve through fourteen. This is the starting point, but how you will fulfill them is dependent on each of the fivefold working together in their own strengths and capacities.

Would it not look strange if my right hand had two thumbs? It would not only look strange, but my hand would not work properly.

I find it fascinating that even in the human body, every single finger is completely unique. It looks different and has a different function and place on the hand. When you use them all together, you become strong.

I wrote down a quick fivefold ministry definition as I have seen it.

> **Fivefold Ministry Definition:** Five appointed leadership positions in the Church, each fulfilling a particular function and flowing in a specific anointing to bring unity and maturity to the body of Christ.

As we look at the church through the generations, we start seeing God doing something. God has started restoring the fivefold ministry to the church.

IS THE FIVEFOLD MINISTRY FOR TODAY?

Chapter 02 – Is the Fivefold Ministry for Today?

Do you know how many people say, "There are no such things as apostles or prophets today"? We are going to look at some of that as we continue along in this book.

Is it not strange though that if you speak about pastors, they say, "Yes, the Church needs pastors"? Even if you speak about teachers or evangelists, everyone agrees that they are needed as well.

So, you have only three fingers on your hand. Why be content with less, when you can have the fullness of what God has given to the Church? Where is the fairness of saying, "There are no apostles for today?"

If you are determined to make that stand, then let's scrap the other four as well to make it even and just call me stumpy.

Which is it going to be? Are you going to believe in the leadership offices or not? You cannot believe in half of them and call that a conviction. I can believe someone that says, "I do not believe in any of them."

In my personal opinion, I will think they are a little off the deep end, but if that is your conviction, you should go with it. Yet, do not say, "I believe in some of them, but not all of them."

Colette Toach

Who are you to decide which half is appropriate and which half is not? It is all or nothing. Perhaps, that is the prophet in me speaking and saying that it is either "black" or "white."

We have a Church that is familiar with the pastoral, teaching and evangelistic offices, but do not tell me that you are familiar with them because of the Old Testament. There were never any evangelists in the Old Testament. Evangelists have a completely New Testament origination.

All or Nothing

So, if you believe that evangelists are for today, then you better believe that prophets are for today as well because they were in the Old Testament. When it comes to the Word, you are all out of excuses.

You are either going to believe it or you are not. You cannot walk a gray line here. You need to take hold of your conviction and walk it out. My conviction is definitely that God did not give only three offices to the Church. He gave all five to lead the rest of the ministries because there are many other ministries listed in Scriptures as well.

The Five Leadership Ministries

Yet, without these five leaders in place, we are not going to see the Church mature.

Ephesians 2:19-21 says,

> *Now, therefore, you are no longer strangers and*
> *foreigners, but fellow citizens with the saints*
> *and members of the household of God,*
> *20 having been built on the foundation of the*
> *apostles and prophets, Jesus Christ Himself*
> *being the chief cornerstone,*
> *21 in whom the whole building, being fitted*
> *together, grows into a holy temple in the Lord,*

There was no mention of apostles in the Old Testament, so we know that what Paul is talking about is the Church in which we exist today. He is saying that the apostles and prophets, with Jesus as the cornerstone, are building the foundation of the Church, so that it might be put together in a place that fits.

It is like Lego blocks. My son loves Lego. Do you know how perfectly those blocks fit together when you are making something? That is a very basic picture of what we are meant to be doing – fitting the pieces together.

The Foundation

First, we have the foundation, which is built by the apostles and prophets with Jesus Himself being the cornerstone. Jesus is the foundation.

We have a bit of an imbalance in the Church sometimes. We have the new move, which centers around the prophets and apostles and so we have our foundation... and that is all we have! On Sundays, we can have a barbeque on our foundation, and on weekdays we can string up some lights on our foundation.

It is just such a pity that we do not have a house to live in. Because if all we believe in is the prophets and apostles, all we have is a foundation.

I sometimes hear, "I am a part of an apostolic church or a prophetic church." Then, all you have is a foundation.

What about the building? Nobody ever went and camped out on a foundation. David did not get a pattern for the foundation. He got a pattern for the temple. Yes, the foundation is the most important because if the foundation is not strong, the rest of the building will crumble.

However, it seems that there is so much emphasis on the foundation that people have forgotten to build the rest of it. This is where the rest of the fivefold ministry comes into play.

We need to build the temple so that we can be fit together. Yet, then we have the other side that fully believes only in building the temple. So they put their bricks right onto the ground.

They do not believe in prophets and apostles. They only believe in the remaining three. Have you ever tried to build anything directly on the soil?

Building Your House on the Sand

When we were in Barbados, we saw that the island consisted of all sea sand. What I found most fascinating was the condition of their roads. They had so many cracks in these roads. I asked our host, "Why are the roads so messed up?"

They said, "The roads are messed up because the sand shifts all the time."

They have to fix the roads very often, because the sand underneath is so loose that it shifts and tears the roads apart. It continually crumbles and they have to fix the roads again and again.

This is how it is in the church today for those that do not believe in apostles and prophets. They have a slab of cement thrown down on the sand, and then wonder why the building is crumbling.

They wonder why there is division, why people are being hurt, why so many people are backsliding, and why the Church is under so much attack. It is because all satan has to do is blow, and that straw house is going to come down - because it has no foundation.

So we see two extremes. It is my personal desire and mandate to bring these extremes to a middle ground, where we have a firm foundation, and each of the fivefold ministry has a place to build this temple.

I love the part in Ephesians that said, "In whom all the building fitly framed together grows…" It is continually growing.

Let the Building Begin!

When you do things right, the sky is the limit. As you establish this pattern that God has for His end-times church, it should continue to grow from glory to glory. Yet, first we have to get everybody into place.

I shared before about the importance of the apostle building his temple. In this book, I want to bring attention to the importance of where you begin to build. Nobody builds a house from the roof down. It does not work.

There is no country or place in this world that I have been to that starts with the roof when they are building a house, and then works their way down to the foundation. They all start with the foundation.

God is doing a new thing, and if we look at the early Church, we will see that the Church was built on a good foundation that lasted for centuries. They were in unity. Yes, the Jews and Gentiles had their odd squabbles, but the apostles got together and made a plan of action.

They set the foundation in place, and that foundation remained. However, what happened next? The apostles died out. Nobody rose up to take their place and the Church started being built on the sand, and slowly, that house started to shift.

Understanding Our Dependency on One Another

Now, it is time that the house of God is built on the rock, and that rock is established by the prophets and apostles with Jesus as the chief cornerstone. If you are an apostle, you cannot do it alone. If you are a prophet, you cannot do it alone.

I do not care which of the fivefold ministry you are - you cannot do it alone. You are just one finger. Maybe you will fulfill one little function, but at the end of the day, it is not you that suffers, it is the body of Christ that suffers.

The body of Christ is suffering right now and is going through lack, disarray, and confusion. I am sure that when you look around, you see things that you would like to change, but the reality is that you cannot change anything by yourself.

The Lord knows that we humans need time to adjust to things, so He started slowly to restore the fivefold ministry. I am not going to go into a major church history lesson, but I think that the move of the pastor was the only ministry that stayed strong.

The Pastoral Ministry

The pastoral ministry is very unique. It has a two-fold function. It has an administrative and a spiritual, anointed function. Some denominations have only one function in place and so they have plenty of administration but the anointing is gone.

According to the correct pattern, the pastor has a two-fold function. If you are looking in the Scriptures, you will see them referred to as shepherds, overseers, and elders. They had more than just administrative functions.

They had an anointing to feed and nurture God's sheep. I do not think that anyone would debate that pastors are meant to be in the church, and that they do indeed exist as part of the fivefold ministry today.

If I look in the Scriptures, James certainly is one of the best pastoral examples. He was an apostolic pastor because he was also an apostle. However, he fulfilled such a pastoral function.

He did not travel out like Peter or Paul. He stayed in Jerusalem.

The Teaching Ministry Restored

Then, we see how God restored the teachers to the church. Spurgeon, Watchman Nee and Andrew Murray are names that you have probably heard of, if you have done any studying.

God started to restore the purity of the teaching office to the church. I am fascinated to see those writings in the last ten years. Though they had been dead for a while, they started to filter through the body of Christ because God started restoring the office of the teacher.

The Lord is doing with us what Paul did to the Gentiles. He is saying, "There is such a thing as a ministry. First, we have the pastor. This is what he does and this is how he looks. Are you ok with that? Now that you are good with that, let me tell you that there is also a teacher."

Watchman Nee had a thriving ministry. He was a powerful man of God and he was a pure teacher. This man was more teacher than pastor, I would daresay. I know that he gave his life for the sheep, but he was really a pure teacher.

If you pick up one of his books, you are going to live it. This is the true sign of a teacher. The Lord started introducing new doctrines and concepts in the church. Read The Normal Christian Life by Watchman Nee and you will see the whole doctrine of sanctification.

The Evangelistic Ministry Restored

This suddenly started spreading through the Church. God was restoring the teaching office. Then, when everyone was comfortable with good teaching, healing evangelists suddenly started popping up everywhere.

They were healing people and raising them from the dead. You could barely get a good night sleep without hearing a revival next door. They were a group of people who no one knew exactly what to call them.

They did not sit still long enough to feed anyone, and they definitely were not teachers. Look at Kathryn Kuhlman. She was a mighty woman of God, but she was no teacher.

I thank the Lord for her healing ministry, but she was not much of a singer or teacher in my personal opinion. John G. Lake was no pastor either. As far as he was concerned, if you went to the doctor, you were going to the devil.

That was not a nice pastoral message. What were people going to call these guys? The evangelistic office suddenly became known in the Church, and then everyone wanted to be an evangelist.

Who wants to be a boring pastor or someone that sits and studies the Word? Those things were boring. Everyone wanted to be an evangelist because they were at revivals performing signs and wonders.

There was all this power, and all of them looked the same. If someone in the teaching era heard of an evangelist, they would call them heretics. They would say that evangelists were not for today.

However, God tends to live by His own rule book, and not by the ones that we try and set. So, He threw the evangelist in, and He got us comfortable with something that was not in the Old Testament, but in the foundation of the early Church that we forgot about when we went through the dark ages.

The Prophetic Ministry Restored

Just when everyone wanted to be an evangelist, God started to breathe into every denomination, and bring to pass the book of Joel, where it said, "And your young men will see visions and your old men will dream dreams."

Suddenly, you have Anglicans wanting to intercede and Baptists having experiences in the Spirit. We are not talking about physical healings and the evangelists. We have people saying, "What is this ministry?"

Clearly, they are not a pastor because their words are "black and white." It is yes or no, up or down, and get right with God. They also are not teachers. Please do not put a prophet behind the pulpit to teach. To preach, yes, but not to teach.

When they get behind the pulpit, they go all over the place and they chase the rabbit when they speak. They are also not evangelists. There are some signs and wonders, but it is not quite the same.

What are we going to call these fellows? Some clever guy must have picked up the Word one day and read Ephesians 4:11 and thought, "Aha. This guy must be a prophet." Then, we saw the prophetic ministry flourish.

Funny enough, a lot more people accepted the prophetic ministry because it was already mentioned in the Old Testament. Yes, there was a lot of confusion on the function of the prophet because the Old Testament and New Testament prophet are not the same.

How can I say that? God added a lot more when He gave the fivefold ministry. He gave a new mandate and a new function. Now, if He gave a new mandate, how could He apply an old pattern?

This is the New Testament, a new covenant. Old things have passed away and all things have become new. This is a latter rain and a new thing God did in His Church.

The function became something new. Yet, if we look in the Old Testament, we will see types and shadows that back up and confirm the new. It was just as Paul did when he discovered the mystery.

Suddenly, there were prophetic words coming from everywhere. The craziest thing is that some denominations do not believe in the gifts of the spirit, but they believe in someone bringing a prophetic word.

They also do not believe that God heals today or that people get visions, but they do believe that there are prophets that can stand up and give a prophetic word. God has restored the prophet to the Church.

People have become comfortable with it across all denominations. It is not uncommon to go to a church and hear the word "prophet," especially in America. They just sprung up. God raised them up out of every denomination.

We reach more prophets in non-charismatic churches in this ministry than in any other denomination because God is doing it, and it is not their great idea. In fact, sometimes, non-Pentecostals make the best prophets because they do not have all the fluff that I grew up with, and we can teach them the right way from the beginning.

They do not go on feelings. They go on the pure Word of God. The prophetic ministry is here to stay whether you believe in it or not.

In the day of Kathryn Kuhlman, you could have said, "I do not believe in evangelists." However, if your daughter was dying, you would be right there at the feet of Kathryn Kuhlman saying, "Pray for me."

God raised her up no matter if you believe in evangelists or not, and regardless of whether you believed in prophets or not. God has raised them up and they have been declaring His word for years.

The Apostolic Ministry Restored

Now, in this very hour, God is restoring the final part of the fivefold ministry. He is now restoring the apostles to the Church.

That move is receiving the same kind of opposition that every other move before it received. You hear, "There is no such thing as apostles for today." On the other hand, you hear the opposite extreme where it feels like everyone is called to be an apostle.

There is no balance. Why is there no balance? It is because the five offices need to be brought together. That is the function of the apostle, and that is why the Lord took the longest to restore the apostle to the Church.

FUNCTIONS OF THE PROPHET AND APOSTLE

Chapter 03 – Functions of the Prophet and Apostle

The Apostle

The apostle goes through the longest time of training. It takes the most planning and living for those that are called. As the Lord has been working on the rest of the fivefold, the apostles have been in the backside of the desert, like Moses and David with the sheep.

Apostles need to be tried and tested. They need to learn to give up everything like Peter did, so that they can be ready for the new move that God is about to bring. Apostle of God, now that you know your call, are you ready to fulfill your purpose?

Are you ready to bring together the fivefold ministry and begin to lay the foundation on which they can build? You are not going to accomplish any of this, if you do not work as a team with the rest of the fivefold.

The apostle did not die out in the New Testament!

There were only twelve apostles, right? That is the argument that you always hear. There are only twelve apostles and they were just for the New Testament church. Those twelve are it. There are no more.

Yet, here in Acts 14:14, I read that Barnabas and Paul were both apostles. They were not part of the twelve. If you are sticking to the theory that there were only twelve apostles and no more, then you are going to have to tear this portion out of the Word.

Also, you are going to have to remove Romans 16:7 because it says,

> *Greet Andronicus and Junias, my kinsmen and my fellow prisoners, who are of note among the apostles, who also were in Christ before me.*

I never heard of these guys, but apparently they were of note among the apostles. So, it is clear that the office of apostle was not just for the twelve, because they spread like wildfire. There were many apostles in the New Testament.

All you have to do is study Apostle Paul's books, and you will see them popping up everywhere. Why was this? It was because the foundation needed to be laid. Jesus came and gave them the pattern because they needed it for the Church at that time.

So, the apostles established the Church of that time and I find it fascinating that those patterns were quite unique. Yet, as the scripture says in Ephesians 2, they jointly fit together.

Read the book of James, any of Paul's books, and also read Peter's, and you will see many different patterns. Some people say, "Why do we even have the book of James? It does not even fit."

Yet, I see an apostolic pattern there. He was a pastor at heart and he worked with the local churches all the time. He was at the headquarters in Jerusalem and he laid a very clear foundation for the rest of the churches to model themselves after.

If you went to the church in Antioch, I guarantee it looked like the church in Jerusalem. It was James' responsibility to make that church what it was. It was his job to lay the foundation.

When you get that concept and you read the book of James, you understand why he says, "This is how I want things done," or "This is how I want you to treat one another."

Then, we look at Paul who was sent to the Gentiles and we see a completely new foundation, but yet it fits with the rest. Then, we have Peter who was sent to the Jews. Once again, somehow, his pattern fits together with the rest as well.

This is what God is doing today. He is raising up apostles, each with a very clear foundation. If we make Jesus the chief cornerstone and connect each foundation to that cornerstone, we will start to establish a temple that fits well together.

The Prophet

What about the prophets? 1 Corinthians 14:37 says,

> *If anyone thinks himself to be a prophet or*
> *spiritual, let him acknowledge that the things*

> *which I write to you are the commandments of the Lord.*

It was for the prophets to interpret and to practically apply the revelation of the apostle. We know that the prophet is called to motivate the body of Christ and to help people find their place in the Church.

How does that apply to working with an apostle? How do you apply that practically? When an apostle has a pattern, it is for the prophet to tell the rest of the Church where they belong in that pattern.

They will go around and say, "Clearly, you are meant to be this piece in the pattern. You over there, you are meant to be a pastor and you will do this portion of this pattern."

It is for the prophet to motivate the church and say, "Look, this is the pattern of our apostle." I love the passage in 1 Corinthians that we just looked at because Apostle Paul says, "Listen to me. You tell me if this is a commandment of God or not. If it is a commandment of God, you better obey it and follow it through."

That is what the prophet is there for. He has the apostle's back. He says, "Yes, that is a commandment of God. I have your back. That is exactly what God is saying. Now, let's get everyone together, get them in place and get them working so that they can fulfill their purpose."

Yet, you have prophets trying to build their own foundations. They are building their houses on sand, or on the other hand, you see them not having any place at all.

So, if you do not have a pattern or a foundation of what your temple should look like, what are you putting people into? How are you helping them reach maturity and fulfill their callings?

Are you just walking around telling people that they are prophets and evangelists? How are you helping them fulfill their place in the pattern? James and Peter made it very clear. His elders knew what to do, and so did his overseers.

They knew who to put where, and that is what the prophets did. The elders in Antioch came in and said, "It is clear that Paul and Barnabas need to be set aside for the work of the Lord. Let us lay hands on them and send them out." (Acts 13:2)

So, all the elders got together and they laid hands on them and sent them out. Prophets are meant to motivate, encourage, put people in their place, and introduce people to Jesus.

Yet, they are meant to do all these things within the context of the pattern of their apostle. If you just get that, it brings a peace. You may be so busy running around trying to fulfill the work that God has given you, yet you feel like something is lacking. You want to know that one day when you leave this world, you have left something behind.

I asked our partners one time, "What do you want to have written on your tombstone one day?" Perhaps this is not the nicest picture, but what one line do you want to epitomize what you have left behind for this generation?

Is it not to establish and build something that will remain? You cannot run around from building site to building site throwing a brick here and another there. You cannot go from ministry to ministry giving your little words saying, "This person belongs here and this person belongs there."

Then, you wonder why people are taking offense? There is nothing wrong with your ministry. You are just not releasing that ministry in the correct context. You need to find the foundation that you are building with your apostle and be at their back.

Building Together

You need to confirm that the revelation they are getting is indeed the Lord. Then, you need to say, "Now, let's look around in this congregation and see where everyone belongs."

It is for the prophets to get revelation, and then it is for them to decree, release, and proclaim the Word of God over that ministry again and again. It is for them to be like Nehemiah who built the walls to protect that city and protect the temple so that it can grow from glory to glory.

Each of us need to fulfill a function, but it is not good enough with only the prophets and apostles. If we do not have the apostles to lay the foundation, what are we going to build on? The sand?

Also, if we do not have prophets to interpret the revelation and help everyone find their place, then how are we going to know where we are going to fit?

FUNCTIONS OF THE TEACHER, PASTOR AND EVANGELIST

Chapter 04 – Functions of the Teacher, Pastor and Evangelist

The Teacher

I love the example of Ezra, who was a teacher, in the Scriptures. After they built the temple, Ezra came and said, "Now that you have your temple, let me teach you how you should be taking care of it." That is what I love about the teaching ministry.

The teacher provides the brick. He comes in and says, "I see that we have a foundation and that everyone is in place, but I also see that everyone does not know how to fulfill their place properly. So, let me take each one of you and teach you how to fulfill your place."

When the temple was dedicated, everyone stood up, glorified the Lord, and then all the scribes and priests went among the people and explained the Word of God to them.

Nehemiah 8:7

> *...and the Levites, caused the people to understand the law, and the people stood in their place.*

I love this picture of the teaching ministry because that is what the teacher should be doing.

Once the pattern is in place and the prophets have given everyone their place, the teacher can come in and say, "Now that you have been given this position, do you know how to fulfill it?

"Let me train you, equip you, raise you to maturity in your call, and help you to understand what it is that you are meant to be doing. Let me give you a sword and teach you how to use it. Let me give you a shield and teach you how to block."

Yet, we have ministers trying to do everything. We have prophets trying to appoint, tell the apostles what to do, and still equip and teach. Prophets make lousy teachers. Do not do it. They are good preachers, but bad teachers.

On the other hand, teachers are good teachers, but bad preachers. Do not try to do the prophetic preaching if you are a teacher. Stick to the Word and do what you are good at. You are the mortar that holds those bricks together. You bring the body of Christ to a place of solidity. You make it strong on that foundation.

The Evangelist

Then, we have the evangelist. I have to share this scripture first. 1 Corinthians 3:9-15 says,

> *For we are God's fellow workers; you are*
> *God's field, you are God's building.*
> *10 According to the grace of God which was*

given to me, as a wise master builder I have laid the foundation, and another builds on it. But let each one take heed how he builds on it.

11 For no other foundation can anyone lay than that which is laid, which is Jesus Christ.

12 Now if anyone builds on this foundation with gold, silver, precious stones, wood, hay, straw,

13 each one's work will become clear; for the Day will declare it, because it will be revealed by fire; and the fire will test each one's work, of what sort it is.

14 If anyone's work which he has built on it endures, he will receive a reward.

15 If anyone's work is burned, he will suffer loss; but he himself will be saved, yet so as through fire.

Do you want a picture of the evangelist? That is it, right there. He is the one that brings the fire. He is the one that says, "You think you are doing so well for God. You think that you are walking as God wants you to walk, but I see that you have a foot in the world and a foot in the church. You think that you can serve God on Sundays and go to the bars on Saturdays?"

These are the hellfire and damnation preachers. You may not like what they say, but you are drawn to listen to them because it brings conviction. That is the role of the evangelist. The teacher comes and teaches each one how to build and how to be a part of that building.

Then, the evangelist comes and says, "You are quite proud of that wall, eh? I can see that you are so proud of your work. Well, let's test it with a bit of fire and see what is left. Let's see how much of it is God, how much is you, how much is the world, and how much is sand."

Then, he brings down the fire and a spirit of conviction. Yes, there are miracles and healings as well, but I am speaking specifically of the ministry that the evangelist has to the Church, not to the world.

Just in case you forgot, Ephesians 4:11 states that God gave these gifts to the church. So, if you do not understand why I am saying that the evangelist is called to the Church, then get the next book in this series.

His first ministry is to bring the fire to the Church. If you hear someone standing about and talking about the world, the devil and sin, then you are more than likely listening to an evangelist.

He is simply bringing some fire to your brick house, so that you can see what will burn and what is left. Is it hay, stubble or gold? Each one has a place. You cannot have a teacher bringing the fire. You can try to spit and spew as a teacher, but it does not burn as much as when an evangelist stands up and brings it.

An evangelist just has a way of releasing that fire upon you with just one word that makes you fall flat on your face and say, "Lord, forgive me. I am a useless sinner." We need more evangelists in the church.

We have everyone running around trying to be whatever sounds good. Yet, each one of them is vital.

The Pastor

Now, we are going to look at the pastor. He is the one that brings order. Sometimes, someone that is building a wall thinks, "I like that guy's wall better than I like my wall. I am going to get involved in his wall and leave mine alone."

The pastor is the one that says, "Is this not your wall? Is this not your place and where God has put you?" The pastor is the one that tends the garden and maintains the order. He has already had the apostle come and set the pattern.

The prophet has given everyone their place, and the teacher has already fully equipped each one. Then, the evangelist comes with the fire and probably gets on the pastor's last nerves.

Just when he thinks that he has a nice calm church, the evangelist comes and throws fire on it and half the church falls to the ground because there was a lot of hay and stubble being thrown around. Then, the pastor has to start all over again and encourage people to rebuild.

The pastor keeps it all together. He needs to flow in all of the gifts of the spirit, because he is the one that reminds each one of their place. He says, "Is this not where the prophet said that you belong? Should you not continue in that place?

Is this not what the teacher said that you should be doing right now? You should be doing that then, right? Do not forget that this is the pattern and direction that we are headed toward as a ministry right now."

He is the one that stays at home. I refer to pastors as spiritual mothers. I refer to them as mothers and not fathers, because the mother is the one that is known to nurture and accept the child for who they are, but yet they invest enough into them so that they become greater than who they are now.

That is the function of a pastor. It is to take someone that has been put in place, has been taught, and then to work with them and nurture them so that they can bring the gold out. Then, when the fire comes, there is no hay or stubble.

The pastor is the one that says, "You have gold in you. Press on and stop looking at everyone else. Stop going here and there." He is the motivator and the nurturer. He reminds them and teaches them day by day.

He says, "This is the doctrine. Do not forget that this is the principle you should base your life on." He feeds them the teaching and gives them a practical way to live. He teaches them how to hold the trowel and where to stand, just like a mother would nurture a child she birthed in the natural.

The mother teaches the child how to brush their teeth, how to flush after they use the bathroom, and how to wash their hands before dinner. This job is very tedious and difficult. I think we need to cut the pastors some slack.

With the rise of the apostolic and prophetic ministries, it is no secret that everyone is out to get those "mean dominating pastors." Yet, you may not realize the function that they fulfill in the Church. We could not have a beautiful house and a temple that is established without their help.

Yet, if that temple is not maintained daily, it will enter into ruin. I daresay that it was the fall of true pastoral ministry that took the Church into the dark ages, because ministry became all about principles and power.

It became about who had the position, and no one had the heart needed to nurture God's people. What the pastor became through that time, is not what the pastor truly is in God's economy.

Now, we see pastors trying to rise up with a true pastoral call, but instead of getting the support that they need, they are getting pushed down because they are "dominating." Some pastors are forced to take a very hard line, because when they did try to nurture and maintain, they faced opposition, attack, and people leaving and talking behind their backs.

So, he had no other choice than to draw a hard line, and then when he does that, everyone says that he is a dominating pastor.

Maintaining the House of God

I am amazed to see that when a house has been standing for a while, it truly looks like it has been standing for a while.

In our home in Mexico, we have some neighbors that have not been in their home for a good number of years. This home is beautiful. They have the pool guy come and maintain it so that there is at least water in the pool.

Yet, I have watched this house month after month and year after year, and though no one has done anything to the house, the paint is starting to peel and weeds have sprung up so that you can barely get into the front door.

There is dust that has coated every part of the house so much that it looks like a thick layer of sludge. When you look at the house, you can feel the spirit of the house. It feels empty and you know that it is going to take a bit of time to restore it.

That is what has happened with our true pastoral ministry in the church. That ministry built a great house in the early Church, but unless it is maintained, lived in, and taken care of, it is just going to slip back again.

Everyone is talking about the restoration of the Church, but God is not restoring the Church. God is building something new. The latter rain is going to be greater than the former rain.

This building is going to be greater because all that we have left from the early Church is the Scriptures. All that we have left is what we can read and remember.

I would have loved to sit down with Apostle Paul about some of his teachings and say, "Explain this to me more. Show me more." Well, today we can do that. As God is raising up apostles, we can stand together and get that pattern for the end-times Church.

This Church is going to be more glorious. Just consider what we have now that they did not have. Firstly, we are around the world. We are not just stuck to a few countries in Asia. We are around the world.

We are spreading the gospel on a daily basis through different kinds of media. We are building a city that is set on a hill. I wonder to myself if Paul, when he talked about the city on a hill, envisioned the Church that we are going to build in this end-times era.

He had his candlestick up that was not hidden under a bushel, but we have way more than a candlestick. We have a city that is high up on a hill, shining in every direction. It carries more than one nation, and reaches more than one denomination.

The Roof That Completes the Building

In 1 Corinthians 12, Paul says that we are the body of Christ, and that Christ has set in place firstly apostles, secondly prophets, and third teachers and also miracles, governments and so on.

After he says all of these things, he says, "Let me show you a better way." After all is said and done, we are at 1 Corinthians 13:1-2. It says,

> *Though I speak with the tongues of men and of angels, but have not love, I have become sounding brass or a clanging cymbal.*
> *2 And though I have the gift of prophecy, and understand all mysteries and all knowledge, and though I have all faith, so that I could remove mountains, but have not love, I am nothing.*

You can build a house made of gemstones and you can build a foundation that is second to none. You can even have a team each fulfilling a fivefold ministry call and you can follow every principle to the letter.

Furthermore, you can even flow in signs and wonders. However, if the roof over your head is not the agape love of Jesus Christ, you are a clanging symbol.

All the work and all the investments you have made are nothing. Without love, you undo all that work because Jesus is the foundation. He, who is love, is also the roof.

At the end of the day, it is not you and I who are keeping this building together. It is Jesus who is keeping it together because it is His temple. Whether you are fulfilling your purpose or not, or whether you know what to do or not, you need to accomplish one thing and that is to make your foundation the agape love of Christ.

If everything that you do is in that love and motivated not by your need, your great vision, but simply by this love, then you truly begin to establish the foundation, the capstone and the roof of the body of Christ.

God is raising up apostles, prophets, evangelists, pastors, and teachers from every denomination. The call is going out for every single one of these warriors to rise up. I declare it even now in the name of Jesus. Rise up and take your place.

THE FIVEFOLD MINISTRY FOR A NEW GENERATION

Chapter 05 – The Fivefold Ministry for a New Generation

> **Romans 8:28** *And we know that all things work together for good to those who love God, to those who are the called according to His purpose.*
> *29 For whom He foreknew, He also predestined to be conformed to the image of His Son, that He might be the firstborn among many brethren.*

This passage is so full I could just share on this for a couple of hours, but I am going to get to the main part that I want to pull out from this.

Before you were born, or even conceived, the Lord knew your name. Not only did He know your name, but He prepared the road that you would walk. He knew that you would be reading this book today.

He knows what you are going to do after reading this book and he knows what you are going to do with the treasures in your life.

Before your parents even knew that you would exist, God had already taken you in the palm of His hand. He looked into your future and He arranged a plan for you to walk out. It is because of this that you stand where you are today.

So often, we try to become what God wants us to be. We try to strive towards this image that we think we need to be. Sometimes you can get so exhausted.

You have this picture in front of you and you think, "One day, I will become this great thing."

You strive, run, and try, but you forget that before you were born, God created in you, the things that you needed to be. He already put all the materials and tools that you would need to become the vessel that He needs you to be.

From the day that you were conceived, He started to make you into that vessel.

I daresay that most of the training that God needs to take you through is not taking you to a new level, but just taking away the junk and revealing what was in you all along.

I discovered this so much later in my own training. I was so busy aiming towards becoming something. However, one day it occurred to me that the roads that God led me down in life, the place I was born, and the life that I had lived, prepared me for the very calling that I am walking out now.

I kept looking for something that I did not have, but I did not realize that I already had the "something" that I needed. God had already predestined and called me. With that in mind, He placed me in situations in my life that would shape my character.

Before I even knew how to call upon His name, my life was being shaped.

Samuel

Even before Samuel knew the voice of his God, his life was being shaped. Before he was born, his mother cried out in the temple and the high priest said to her, "Next year this time, you will have a son."

Before all of that took place and she conceived, Samuel's ministry was already mapped out. Before he knew the sound of the voice of his master, God had already started arranging his circumstances so that he would be one of the greatest prophets of our time.

His words did not fall to the ground. God took him from his mother and put him in the temple. That very life experience shaped him in a way that nothing else could have shaped him.

It made him into the prophet that he became.

Had Samuel been raised at home or anywhere else, I doubt that he would have been the prophet that we saw rising up in the house of Eli.

However, God had a plan. Before Samuel was born, God started shifting his life to gear him towards the calling that he would walk out one day.

When you come to terms with that, you come to the powerful revelation of His grace. You do not need to strive to "become." That is the easy part. The most difficult part is learning to discover what God has already put in you.

Right now, there is so much junk on top of the call that you have lost sight of what God already started in you from the beginning. You see, every single experience that you have faced in life has geared you towards your ministry call.

Yeah, it is very likely that you made some wrong decisions and went down some wrong roads. Yet, have you not also experienced where somewhere down the line you end up in a ministry situation or something and you can draw on the roads that you have already walked?

You suddenly say, "Thank you Lord that I walked down those roads because it equipped me to do what I am doing now."

Looking Back

I had some crazy desires as a child. I wanted to become an English teacher. In my mind, language teachers had the greatest effect on all the kids. I thought, "It would be so nice to train people and have an effect on their lives."

I did not become an English teacher, but the desire that was in me is still there. I also wanted to become an air hostess. I wanted to fly and see the world. I wanted to go out. I felt limited where I grew up in South Africa.

That was not something that I got from my parents when I was growing up. Although my father moved around a lot, he would have been happy to just stay in one place.

He always said, "Where do you get this crazy idea from?"

"I don't know. I just have this desire."

I look at that child back then and I see this germ call. There is a lot of junk that I decided to pile onto those desires and some ways that I thought I should walk them out. However, if I strip all the junk away and look at the germ thought, I see that from the time I was born, God was gearing me for what I am doing right now.

It has shaped me, changed the way I think, and it has geared me for the future and what I am doing. It has prepared me for my own team and for my entire ministry. If I look back through my life, I can identify these checkpoints all along the way.

God was edging me from experience to experience.

Yes, not all the choices that we made were righteous. Yet, somehow God even managed to reach into those circumstances, yank us out, and pull us through. Even in the times when you were not saved and you did not know Him, you look back and see the hand of God in your life.

Look at Your Journey

You see, if you had not taken that job, moved to that specific place, or taken that step, you would not know Him as you do today.

Before you were born, He already started to gear you for this call on your life. That brings a peace. You do not need to strive to "become." You just need to look at the germ call that He has already put inside of you.

When you can do that, then it is a time to build. Yes, the ministry trainings are going to come and shape you, but what I am going to look at in this chapter is that this is something that God has geared you for your entire life.

Through your successes, failures, life-experiences, and relationships, God has used it all to bring you to the point where you are right now.

How God Trains His Leaders

What I am going to do is explain a bit on what God does to train His fivefold ministers.

Once you have seen what God has taken you through, I want to show you that because of what you have experienced in life, you are able to use these skills and abilities on all three roads.

You probably are so focused and zoomed in on one part of your life that you are not seeing the bigger picture. You are not seeing how God has made you complete.

So, you know now that God will take you through a preparation phase of your calling, which includes life-experiences. We often refer to this as ministry preparation.

Ministry Preparation Defined

This is what God does to gear you for your call. He brings certain life-experiences on you until you reach a place where you are ready to accept the call on your life.

When you are ready to accept that call, He will take you to what we call the training phase. Preparation is the longest because we, humans, are stubborn. We don't get the lesson the first time around.

We are like the children of Israel. We have to go around the mountain twenty times before we get it right.

How many times have you faced the same circumstance and messed it up every time? Then finally, you get it right.

When you finally get that out of the way, go through those life-experiences, and face the tests that you need to face, you come to a season where God zeroes in and focuses you in a particular direction.

With this focus comes a specific training. I am going to cover the fivefold ministry and what the training looks like for each one. I will also share the qualities it brings out of you.

The spiritual qualities are obvious, so I am going to skim over those because I will go into detail for each one, in the rest of the series.

I have come to realize that these trainings do not just bring forth anointing, but a change in character. Anyone that has gone through a ministry training, knows what I am talking about.

The Lord will say, "It is not good enough that you are so bold. You need to learn to love."

"It is not enough that you love. You need to learn to be bold."

Where you were as meek as a mouse, you need to roar like a lion. The Lord does not just leave you alone. You have so much potential inside, but your character needs to change so that potential can be released.

A Look at Character Training

That is the part that we have not looked at much when we speak about ministry training. We have talked about the face-to-face with Jesus, flowing in the anointing, and the various gifts of the Spirit, but what about the character change it takes you through?

You will be interested to discover that the character traits that are brought out of each of the fivefold ministry are quite distinct.

Why is that?

It is because in order for that specific anointing to flow, to achieve that kind of function in the Church, you need to become a certain kind of person. You need to have a character change to flow that way.

If I am going to be a mother, I better act like one. I cannot act like a father and try to be a mother. You need to become the character of the ministry that you are going to fulfill. It is very distinct for each of the fivefold.

In the chapters that follow I am going to outline some of this for you. While I do teach on the specific training for each of the fivefold ministry here, I am taking you to the finish line.

This book is about giving you a picture of what the fivefold ministry looks like in the Church, and there is no better way to illustrate this than to paint a picture for you of someone that has already gone through the process.

The Need for Training

What many do not realize is that when the scripture below tells us to "study" to show ourselves as approved, is that Paul was talking about a lot more than buying this book in the hopes of cementing your call!

> **2 Timothy 2:15** *Be diligent to present yourself approved to God, a worker who does not need to be ashamed, rightly dividing the word of truth.*

The word "study" here is defined as such in the Strong's Concordance:

4704

endeavor 3, do diligence 2, be diligent 2, give diligence 1, be forward 1, labor 1, study 1; 11

1) to hasten, make haste

2) to exert one's self, endeavor, give diligence

In other words, it is going to take a lot more than getting a decree to fulfill a fivefold ministry function in the church. It means going through a season of diligence and pushing through the training to show yourself approved! This kind of training is something only the Holy Spirit can take you through.

If you have a fivefold ministry calling, then you are nodding your head in agreement, because you have already faced the fires and the training that comes with being given such a call. From the moment you are called to be a pastor, pressure comes at you from all sides.

Called to be a prophet? You probably got kicked out of your church (or left) and if you are a teacher, what you thought you understood, just became a massive confusion.

Why this sudden shift when the Lord confirms your call? It is so that you might go through the refining process that Peter speaks about in 1 Peter 1:6-7

> *In this you greatly rejoice, though now for a little while, if need be, you have been grieved by various trials,*
> *7 that the genuineness of your faith, being much more precious than gold that perishes, though it is tested by fire, may be found to praise, honor, and glory at the revelation of Jesus Christ*

Is your faith genuine? Is your call true? It is only once you have passed through the fire that you truly discover the gold so beautifully deposited inside of you by the Holy Spirit.

So yes, along with this calling comes a season of preparation and training. Just as David was prepared in the sheepfold and then trained in the courts of Saul, so also does the Holy Spirit take each of the fivefold ministry through a season of training to hone them into weapons of mass destruction!

Each one is a vital part of what He needs to do in the Church. You should not be surprised then to discover that because of the clear distinction between each of the ministries, that the training is diverse as well.

Why? Well simply put, if I wanted to train an athlete to run 100m sprints, I would give him quite a different workout to someone I would want to train for a wrestling match.

Ministry Specific Training

Each requires a different skill set and muscle strength. Is one inferior to the other? Not at all, they simply have their own race to run! The same is true for the fivefold ministry. Each is a vital part of the Church, but quite diverse in their function.

This is why they go through their own seasons of training. The training that the Holy Spirit takes an evangelist through does not look anything like the training a teacher goes through. It should be clear to you, why it has to be that way. The evangelist is going to call down fire and tackle demons, while the teacher is called to renew the minds of God's people.

Like anyone in the body of Christ, they will function in all of the gifts of the Spirit, however how these gifts manifest through their ministry will differ greatly, simply because of their defined purpose in the Church.

Now you cannot go through this kind of preparation and training without your character being shaped. A large portion of your training will be spiritual. It is meant to equip you to function in the gifts and anointing as you should. However, the greatest change does not come during that part of your training!

The change comes as the Holy Spirit begins to form in you, the character you need to fulfill the function you are called to in the Church.

What many do not realize is how permanent this change is. Depending on your call, your very character, traits, likes, archetypes, and desires will be changed by the hand of God. Consider how when you were unsaved your desires were all centered around sinning.

A Complete Renovation

Now that you serve the Lord, your re-created spirit desires to please the Lord and fulfill His call on your life! His desires became your desires. You have desires and ambitions in you today that you did not have before you were saved.

I was never the maternal type, so when the Lord gave me four natural children, and then called me to be a spiritual mother to countless others, I was stumped! I said, "Then Lord you need to give me the heart for this!" He was so faithful. Today I look at those He has brought to me and the love I feel for each one overtakes me!

I have to say, "That is God!" That is what it means to walk in His power and not your own. This desire did not just effect my ministry - it changed my life.

In the same way, as the Holy Spirit comes upon you to bring about this change, it is going to do a lot more than just make you more anointed. It is going to change who you are as a person. That is why in the chapters that follow I am going to talk about the character of the fivefold ministry.

I want you to realize that when someone has gone through the refining fire, as Peter talked about, that the gold that rises up from that is quite distinct.

The gold that gleams in the evangelist is a beacon in the dark! The reflected face of Jesus in the pastor is evidence of the dross that was burned away in his life.

You can look at someone who has been through that refining fire and say with certainty, "Yes, I see that your character has been shaped by the Holy Spirit! You have the character of a prophet through and through!"

The Preparation Phase

There are two phases that the Holy Spirit will take each one that has a calling through. The first is the preparation and as the name dictates, this gets you geared towards your call. This preparation starts at conception and before you even knew of your own existence, the Lord reached down and called you His own.

Like I already shared, He arranged the circumstances you were born into and then further arranged to save you from them. The roads you walked prepared you for this calling on your life, and led you to this point, where you stand right now.

Certainly, you chose some wrong roads along the way, but the Lord was so faithful, wasn't He? It was as if you were drawn as a magnet time and again to this point. You tried to outrun it, and found that call waiting for you at the finish line.

You tried to ignore it, and it woke you in the middle of the night. You tried to feign ignorance and the Lord would send you someone to give you a word of confirmation. In fact, if you were to look back over your life, you will see the hand of the Lord nudging and sometimes shoving you, in the direction that you need to go.

That is the nature of our Savior. Meditate for just a moment on this beautiful Psalm to understand everything that the Lord has gone through to prepare you for the road ahead.

Psalm 139:13-18

> *For You formed my inward parts; you covered me in my mother's womb.*
> *14 I will praise You, for I am fearfully and wonderfully made; marvelous are Your works, and that my soul knows very well.*
> *15 My frame was not hidden from You, when I was made in secret, and skillfully wrought in the lowest parts of the earth.*
> *16 Your eyes saw my substance, being yet unformed. And in Your book they all were written, the days fashioned for me, when as yet there were none of them.*

17 How precious also are Your thoughts to me, O God! How great is the sum of them!
18 If I should count them, they would be more in number than the sand; when I awake, I am still with You.

His hand covered you while you lay in your mother's womb. His thoughts followed you through life. His heart has lead you to this point and even now, His Spirit continues to shape and prepare you.

You cannot help but be transformed during this process. This phase that I have called "preparation" has a single purpose – to bring you to a point of conviction. To lead you to the stark reality of, "The Lord has called me for His good will and purpose."

When you look over your life, study your convictions and seek God, you look up with a new truth in your heart. You are called. You have a purpose. From the moment you embrace this truth, you are ready to move onto the next phase. The phase that will forge you into the minister He has called you to be.

The Training Phase

After Paul's conversion and call to ministry, we still see much of the "core" passion God has placed in him from birth. However along with it, we see some definite changes as well. One who is willing to lay his life down for his friends.

Instead of following the Sanhedrin blindly, we see a man who began to establish a pattern for the entire New Testament Church. He set out a structure that had never been seen before. He did not just raise up disciples – he appointed elders and trained up spiritual sons!

As he rose up out of Arabia we find a character formed in him that he did not have before! This season of training is what takes everything you have faced in preparation and shakes loose the junk that you added to your call.

As a result, the true nature that God intended for you begins to surface through the dross. From there, new traits are added to you that you simply never had. It is these traits that remind us that we are called because of His grace and not because of our own works and talents.

As you put these two aspects together, you are given a clear picture of your call. As I begin from the next chapter, to outline the character of each of the fivefold ministry, I need you to understand a few things.

The first thing is that I am not describing a natural character trait for each. Rather I am outlining for you, what the character of each ministry looks like after training! Although preparation might have led them towards this call, it is the training that the Holy Spirit takes them through that infuses them with something that they did not have before.

So for example, just because your natural temperament is amiable and you like people, does not mean that you are a pastor! However, if God has called you to be a pastor, you can be sure that He is going to shape your character to have a heart for His people.

I hope that I am making this clear and that you pay keen attention to separating the natural temperament of someone and their ministry character that has been forged through the heat of the flame.

THE FIVEFOLD MINISTRY CHARACTER

Chapter 06 – The Fivefold Ministry Character

The Evangelistic Character

The first thing that an evangelist goes through is a season of developing a relationship with the Holy Spirit. It is not about intimacy. It is not nice with rose petals and sweetness. It is about power and the external anointing.

There is going to be conviction, healing, bringing down the glory of God, and demons manifesting.

When you go through this kind of training, it strips your strengths completely. It leaves you dependent on the Holy Spirit alone.

When an evangelist starts going through this kind of training, they become very sensitive to the work of the enemy. They become very angry when they see God's people bound.

They are very angry when they see the lost in bondage. They want to reach into the fire and snatch them out. They are passionate people.

I love to see when the Lord takes a nice amiable person that does not like to be confrontational and says, "I have called you to be an evangelist."

When I see that happen, I think, "You are about to go through a character change because you cannot get angry at the devil quietly."

You cannot say to the devil nicely, "Demon, we need to talk about you moving. I know that you are comfortable, but please can you go?"

No! There is nothing amiable about the evangelist. You cannot be nice. It is black or white. There is a strong conviction. Being that it is like this, you become discontented with the way things are.

You are not happy with lukewarm in the church. You want to see hot or cold. You can work with an unbeliever that is dead and cold. Your heart is passionate for that.

"Give me somebody that is completely in the world, a pagan and a sinner. I can work with that."

"Give me a Christian who is on fire. I can work with that."

"Do not give me someone who is complacent, sitting in the back seat of the church, thinking that they have all the answers."

That is the heart of an evangelist. They have a fire. Sin is sin and righteousness is righteousness. There is no middle line.

You will see a lot of similarity between the prophet and the evangelist. Yet, the evangelist definitely draws a much harder line with a strong emphasis on the external and the flowing of the Holy Spirit.

They also have a strong emphasis on demons, identifying sin, and pulling out the spirit of the world. They are the hellfire, and damnation preachers. You either love them or hate them, but they are needed in the body of Christ.

They are the ones that bring revival and set the church on fire because they are not content to be complacent.

To be able to flow in that kind of anointing, you have to go through a character change. You cannot confront and set people on fire quietly. If you are a quiet kind of person, you are going to have to change.

If you have watched any evangelist, you will notice that their nature is one thing, but when they stand up to minister, they're something completely different. They have to go through that character change.

They have to be angry at the enemy and hate sin. They have to see the one little spot on the white sheet and hate it. That is the heart and passion of the evangelist. That training that God takes them through gears them towards that.

A Challenger

One of the qualities that the evangelist develops in his training is to become a challenger. They will not allow you to just sit in one place. They will challenge holy living. They will challenge you to the next level.

They will say, "It is not good enough to just be at this level. You need to go deeper. You need to be more clean and righteous."

There is no left or right. There's just one straight line down the middle. We are taking that line and there is no going around the bend. They don't just accept things the way that they are.

They tend to stir the pot and make people uncomfortable.

Fearless

They also learn to become fearless. They are fearless because their training strips them so much of themselves that they come to depend on God alone. There is nothing in themselves that they can boast in.

They cannot say, "The Holy Spirit comes because I pray so much or because I am so righteous."

They come to a place of such dependence on the Holy Spirit that makes them fearless. Have you ever heard of some of the crazy things that God asks evangelists to do?

You think, "Wow! You must really have some guts and really be able to hear from God."

They have gone through a training, a stripping and shaping, by the hand of the Holy Spirit that has brought them to a place where it is "all or nothing."

"If God tells me to stand on one foot and cluck like a chicken, then that is exactly what I am going to do. Obviously, He has a plan."

As a result, they are risk takers. They are not afraid to step out and open their mouths.

Everybody dances around uncomfortable situations. Yet, an evangelist will jump right in and say, "Why aren't you serving God? Why are you dating that unbeliever when you know that it is against the Word?"

Cause and Effect

A good example of this is Philip, the evangelist. He brought action each time that he preached. That is what the evangelist achieves. They bring action and repentance.

By the time you are finished listening to an evangelist, you want to do something. You either want to repent, evangelize, or something. You cannot just sit middle of the road. You feel that you have to do or be something.

To bring that kind of anointing, you have to become that kind of person. When you look at those qualities, perhaps you can imagine for yourself how such a person would function in both business and ministry.

Don't you see that when you allow the Holy Spirit to take you through these trainings on the ministry side, He is not only giving you an anointing, but shaping your character for success?

God has shaped you for a purpose and it is not only for one part of your life, but for each part. When you see that, it blows everything wide open.

An evangelist is a bringer of conviction. You cannot just stay content around such a person. That is what the training achieves in an evangelist.

The Pastoral Character

Anyone that has gone through pastoral training knows the first thing that they learn. This training will stretch you beyond what you can do.

The pastor has a dual position. One is a ministry position and the other is an administrative position. He is a leader of the Church, but also needs to pour out in ministry.

The training that a pastor goes through is quite intense. I am not talking about pastor, as in position, but as a part of the fivefold ministry. Perhaps, I should use the word shepherd. This would give you a clearer picture of what I am talking about.

This is not a pastor in an administrative sense, but one in context of the fivefold ministry.

God will stretch you beyond what you can do. He will do this so that you can become a leader. In order to be a good shepherd, you need to know where to lead the sheep and where the good pasture is.

All Things to All Men

As a result, you need to become all things to all men. You need to know a little bit about everything. You need to be a leader and be capable. You need to love in one breath and correct in the other.

You need to be able to reach every kind of person. You need to be able to reach out to the lost and to the believer alike. Your ministry is going to be very varied. However, most of all, you are going to be like a mother to the church.

A good picture of what a pastor should be is the role of a mother to a young child. He nurtures. He takes the teaching and doctrine and breaks it up into little pieces.

You know how a mom prepares food for a baby? She does not take a huge steak and slap it in front of a two-month-old baby. You need to give the child some time to grow. Give them some mushed up apples a bit at a time.

They will spit it out and the mom will try to feed them again and again. They will finally get to a point where they will eat the whole thing. That is the role of the pastor.

Sometimes you want to say, "This pastor is so boring. He just keeps spoon feeding me."

He is fulfilling his ministry call. Give the guy a break. That is what he is meant to be doing.

The teacher is the one with the steak, but the pastor takes that steak and cuts it up and feeds it to the people so that it is easy to chew.

In order to be this kind of person, you have to change who you are. Becoming a pastor is not an easy task. It was probably one of my most challenging trainings because I learned that I had to actually be nice.

The Lord said to me, "You are going to have to be nice to people. You are going to have to listen to their problems and you are going to have to care. I need you to love my people and be a mother."

It was through that training that I learned to progress and become a spiritual mother. I needed to learn to nurture and have positive expectation of everyone that the Lord brought me.

Being a Shepherd

I had to feed them by hand, like a shepherd with a lamb. He takes the lamb that cannot keep up with the other sheep and he is there helping it to find its way. To become this kind of person means changing who you are.

You learn to become capable and to take on more responsibility than you should. When you become a mother for the first time, you think, "Wow. I never knew that I could survive on so little sleep and still do so much."

You are pushed to your limits and to the boundary of your sanity. Yet, you still survive. You look back and think, "How on earth did I do that?"

There is something about that responsibility that pushes you beyond what you thought you can do. It makes you capable.

A Capable Leader

Someone who has been through pastoral training is a leader. They know how to host. They are thinking five steps ahead of everyone else. They are aware of everyone's needs.

They know who is going through a hard time and who is not going through a hard time. Their character is one of continually imparting knowledge and always being there.

They are the counselors and the ones that listen and take the children on the knee.

To flow like this, you have to become loving and tender. You have to become the type of person that people feel comfortable around.

You know when you are around a real pastor. You can sit with such a person and share your whole life with them. You can just stay there for hours and be with them. You feel so at peace. This is a real pastor.

That is the quality that this training will put in you. It will pull things out of you that you never knew were there. It will start shaping you to think of others first, before yourself.

You will not be shouting about bringing down the fire or about having more glory. You are not like the evangelist.

Peacemaker

You are the one saying, "Let's go to the gentle stream. Let's get a picnic blanket right here where there is a sweet anointing. Let's chat a little. Share your heart with me. I will give you some counsel."

Can you see why this was such a stretch for me?

It is one of the most challenging trainings, but it is powerful. When you can flow like that, you can reach anyone. That is what a real pastor looks like.

You want your pastor to be something more. You want him to be a fiery preacher or something, but that is not his nature.

Do you not understand that in order to fulfill that function in the Church, to continue to feed a bit at a time, has its place?

We Need One Another

Now, if you leave out the rest of the fivefold ministry, that will bring an imbalance in the church. That is what we are seeing.

There are people who are calling themselves pastors, but they are really evangelists. So, everyone must go out and win the lost. Everyone must have an emphasis on sin and must get born again and again every Sunday.

"If there is nobody that is lost at the meeting, then the congregation must come up for the altar call because otherwise, I look bad."

It is all about fire and "More Lord, more Lord."

Someone is in the congregation thinking, "I am having marital problems, I am struggling with my children, and I have problems at work. How do I deal with these things?

The fire feels great, but I need to nibble on a snack. Fire, waterfalls, and all this fluff is not doing it for me. I am trying not to do anything sinful and to live for God, but somehow I am still struggling."

That is why we need our pastors. They are the ones that give us the practical steps 1, 2, and 3.

They say, "Tell me what happened."

"Alright. Do you see what's going on here? This is what the Word of God says. Give this a try and get back to me."

They are someone that you can share your heart with. We need both in the body of Christ. It is good to have the day to day principles as well as the fire. We need both. They balance each other out.

However, since you have a single focus, you look at the other fivefold ministry members and think, "Why can they not be more like me? Why don't they have my fire?"

Uniqueness of the Fivefold

They are not meant to have your fire.

That training takes them through a complete character change. I love to see when the Lord takes someone that is so not pastoral and calls them to be a pastor.

You just see this look on their face, "You are kidding me, right?"

"Rather tell me that I am unsaved and that I have missed God completely. Anything but be a pastor!"

If the Lord has called you to any of the other fivefold ministries, you will have to go through at least the evangelist or the pastor first. So, if you thought that you could escape that, you are wrong.

The Internal Anointing

The pastor flows in an internal anointing. It is a gentle anointing. He brings you into the presence of the Prince of Peace. It is like a healing anointing. It saturates you with healing inside and out.

It is like a restful, gentle stream. You come to realize that God is your healer, emotionally, physically, and spiritually. He brings you to peace. Being that he does this, he also is the one that gives people a place to belong.

He brings unity because when you come to peace and everyone else comes to peace, unity starts to develop. That is one of the greatest functions that he fulfills in the Church, the bringing of unity.

An evangelist is the one that says, "If you love your mother and brother more than the Lord, you are not worthy to follow Him. He will bring division between the sons and fathers..."

That is the evangelist right there. He is ready to divide, cut, die, and burn the lot to the ground.

We need that from time to time. We need the getting rid of the dross moments.

However, the pastor is saying, "Let's have a look at this situation. Let's see how we can bring peace and give counsel. Let's see how we can gain some understanding. Let me give you some principles to live by daily."

Each ministry has its place. The evangelist and pastor are two very extreme characters. This is why when the Lord starts to switch you between these two, it can be very confusing.

Perhaps you can identify phases where God has said to you, "Ok, stop being this. I need you to be this."

It was because He needed you to go through a character change so that you could accomplish your call. The fivefold ministries are just steps toward your calling and vision. The great thing about these trainings is that they shape your character.

The Teacher's Character

The teacher has a deep relationship with the Word. A great part of his training is the renewing of the mind.

Problem Solver

He is someone that really knows how to learn, causing him to become a solution bringer. One quality that I think is fantastic in a teacher is that he is a really good troubleshooter.

The Lord takes the teacher aside and makes them dig into the Word. So, they learn to learn. They do not just know how to study. I am not talking about someone that can quote the Bible.

This is not about someone who calls themselves a teacher because of how many scriptures they can quote.

I want to know how many scriptures you can teach and feed to God's people. Giving chapter and verse does not make you a teacher. You just know the Word well. Anyone can do that.

It takes a real teacher to live the Word, know the Word, and then feed the Word to others. You cannot have one without the others. A teacher has done all three.

Overcomer of Trials

Many of us know the Word, but a teacher is one, through his training, that has gone through difficult life-experiences and could not find the answers. So, he started digging, crying out, and saying, "God, I need answers."

He gets into the Word and listens to every teaching that he can get his hands on.

He says, "Lord, why am I poor? Why am I sick? Why is my wife leaving me and why doesn't anybody like me?"

He is so sick of it all and he gets into the Word. He starts reading books and goes to seminar after seminar. He cries, begs, and learns.

He finds a bit of truth from this teaching and a bit from another teaching.

He finds a passage and says, "That is fantastic. That answers this question. If I apply this principle and take hold of that other principle, I am starting to see a solution come together for my problem."

They work their way through. When they face a marital problem, they say, "Lord, give me answers."

They will start digging in the Word and then they will bump into someone that shares a principle with them.

"There is something about that principle. It reminds me of that teaching in the Word. I can see where I am failing in my marriage right now. I need to fix this."

They fix it and they work their way to a solution. They see it in the Word, and because of that, they can teach it.

Living Knowledge

When you sit under a teacher like that, you will live what they teach. If you have a prophetic calling and you pick up any of our prophetic books, you will live what we teach.

It will strike you right in the heart. You can speak to any of our students about that. You will live what we teach because it is not just about chapter and verse. It is about living the Word. It becomes a double edged sword, living and breathing.

A teacher does not ever let up. God will not let you let up. He will even take away the principles that you had, the things that always worked.

When God takes you through teacher training, He will strip those principles from you.

You will say, "I know the answer to that. You can just do..."

"What happened? This worked before! God, why is this not working?"

He wants to teach you another way, just to make a point. He wants you to stay teachable and realize that it is not about your principles. It is about your ability to get His wisdom, day by day.

That is the kind of training that a teacher goes through. It is a time of being confused, and a renewing of the mind.

What qualifies a good teacher?

They have lots of problems.

They have lived life to the fullest and have overcome using the Word. This shapes their character.

When they see heresy in the church, they get angry. They are angry because they know the truth and have lived the truth.

When there is someone that is sick and someone stands up and says, "It's God's will for you to die," they get angry.

They say, "That is not what I have learned from the Word. That is not the God that I came to know."

They want to get in there and teach the truth. They are not complacent to just take everything.

They know how to use knowledge and because of that, like I said, they are fantastic troubleshooters. They think differently. They learn to operate in wisdom like none of the other fivefold ministry do.

Hungry for Truth

They may not always have a quick answer, but when you go to a teacher, he will find you an answer. You will be able to ask him anything. If he does not have the answer, he will find it for you. He knows how to find answers. He knows how to learn.

That is the change of character that God takes a teacher through. He makes him think beyond himself. He presses his experiences and knowledge to the boundary and beyond.

When I was going through this training, I felt like God emptied me so much. I was stuck against problems that I really did not know the answers to.

I said, "Lord, give me an answer."

"Go and find it."

"Lord, give me an answer."

"Go and find it."

"Lord, give me an answer!"

"You are really not listening to me. I am not giving you the answer. You will go and find it."

I prayed, travailed, and threw a tantrum or two and then I got into the Word.

I said, "Lord, I will not stop reading the Word until I get my answer."

I read and read and read and then... I found my answer!

Faith Through the Word

I learned to reach out in faith and take, through the scriptures, what I needed to feed myself with. The awesome thing was that when I took hold of that, it was like taking hold of a foundation that I could impart to others.

It changed my character.

For prophets, it is cool. You come into the presence of the Lord and ask for revelation and the Lord gives you the answer. You become lazy.

I was so lazy. I just wanted to pray and get revelation. I did not need to "think." I did not need intelligence or knowledge. I used to say, "You do not need knowledge, just wisdom."

Knowledge and Wisdom

That was before teacher training when I discovered that Solomon really talked about knowledge a lot as well as wisdom. I discovered how important is was to not just have knowledge, but the right kind of knowledge so that you can impart it to others.

It really changes the way that you see things. It means not accepting things the way they are.

A teacher works through problems. Since things did not come easy, he has a "bite like a bulldog" attitude. He says, "We are going to push through, seek God, and get into the Word, until we find a solution."

This makes his feet so firmly grounded that he is not easily moved.

"The Word of God says this. It has always come through for me. I am not moving."

It makes a very stable person. Anyone that knows a true teacher, knows what I am talking about. There is something about their character that you feel secure about. They have it together and they are stable.

They may be passionate in what they present and may even have different temperaments, but their character is one that shows that they know what they are talking about.

Lived What They Know

They have lived their message and you feel secure when you are listening to them, because they feel secure teaching. You feel comfortable.

You say, "I see where you are coming from."

They bring peace.

The teacher opens eyes and they change the way people think. I love that part of the teaching anointing. It renews your mind and gives you a foundation to build on.

Those are, in essence, the traits that the teacher training will develop in you.

The Prophetic Character

What about the prophet? I have an entire series called The Prophetic Field Guide series on the prophet, so I will give you the bottom line here.

The training for the prophet brings you into a face-to-face relationship with Jesus. It strips you of all your strengths and weaknesses. It brings you to a reality of death and an understanding of the power of resurrection.

It is an up and down journey. Just when you are a little puffed up, you are brought down. When you are down and think that you are useless, you are brought up.

You think, "Lord, make up your mind. Either you are going to crush me or raise me up high, but this is getting me down."

Welcome to prophetic training. What else were you asking for?

When you are high in your own opinion, you are leveled. When you hide your head under your pillow, doubting your salvation, the Lord tells you to speak a word to someone.

You think, "Are you kidding? Right now, I need a word. I need ministry!"

That is the walk of the prophet. He is to be dependent on God alone and have a face-to-face relationship with Jesus.

Strength From a Point of Brokenness

There is something about being so broken yourself that gives you compassion for the broken and rejected. If I had to take just one quality or character trait that God develops in the prophet, I would have to say that the prophet is the motivator.

He is the one saying, "I know that you are full of it and you have failed. I know that you are broken, rejected, and a loser, but you can do it.

I was also broken, rejected, and a failure. I was lost and God picked me up. He dusted me off and took away the rough edges and put me where I am today. If He did it with me, He can do it with you."

The prophet is the one that sees the guy in the corner that is unnoticed. He sees him because he was once the guy in the corner that was unnoticed. It develops character to notice the rejected, broken, and wounded.

You were so wounded and broken yourself. Can you not see that God has geared you for this your whole life?

This has developed a certain character in you. It is not just because you are amiable or a nice guy. It is simply because you have been there. You know what it is like. Since you know what it is like, you have a heart of love.

Being that the prophet has this character, he is able to break down walls. He can bring the gentle breeze of Jesus, the internal anointing that heals the brokenhearted.

Out of all of the fivefold ministry, the prophet flows in inner healing the most. It is so because they needed healing the most.

Show me a prophet and I will show you someone whose life has been broken and built up many times. You will see in that person a character that has compassion. They cannot handle unrighteousness.

They cannot handle seeing someone in the Church downtrodden and ignored.

I remember this particular event when we were in Switzerland. After a meeting, we had a dinner together in a restaurant. The leaders were all at this big table.

I looked over and saw someone that could not afford to eat at this restaurant. Everyone else was there so they did not want to miss out. They just sat there with a glass of water.

I could not bear it. I went to the leaders and said, "Can we not invite them?"

"Yes, sure."

Then, I saw another one in the corner.

"Hey, do you think we can just add one more person?"

At the end, our table was packed with everyone there.

I have been the one that was sipping on a glass of water. I know how it feels to be there because you know that this is where God wants you to be, but you are uncomfortable and humiliated.

I could not bear seeing someone else go through what I went through. I just wanted to make it better.

"Come on! Everyone can be a part of the leadership table."

I do not know how popular I was, but that is the heart of the prophet. They have been through those experiences and they know how it feels. For this reason, they are the motivators.

They are the ones saying, "You can do it. You can break free. You have a place in the body of Christ. Jesus is there for you."

The Apostolic Character

What about the apostle? I find it hard to define the training of the apostle in just a few short points. I would say that this training breaks away what you thought you were and makes you into the image of Jesus.

Becoming the Image of Christ

You are added to so much. God tears you down to your core, that little germ call. He takes away your anointing, principles, friends, family, strengths, and everything else.

Then you say, "Lord, what's left?"

He says, "The tiny little bit left… that is me!"

"Lord, there is nothing left."

"Look deeper. Do you see that tiny little gold coin of treasure in you? That is me."

He takes that treasure and He starts to build on it. He causes you to see things that you did not see before. He starts adding to you, one step at a time. However, first comes the tearing down part and then the building up part.

Since you have been so stripped and you had to go through so many experiences, your eyes are open. You see roads and people that you never saw before. You no longer have those preconceived ideas and walls that you have built up through the years.

You are not going to have a clear vision and view of the future if He does not tear you down first. I am just talking about the personal change you go through. I am not talking about your function in the body of Christ.

A New Creation

If you see how the Lord breaks the apostle down and adds to them in their own lives, you will see how that naturally flows towards ministry and functioning as an apostle in the church.

You have your preconceived ideas of what the Church should be. You have all your life-experiences and you have made up your ideas of what you think should happen.

God has to strip that all down because underneath all of that lies one little piece of truth. All the rest is added garbage. You are not seeing His pattern. You stole some pieces from everybody.

You are not seeing what He wants you to see, so He tears everything down. Then, one piece at a time, like a master architect designing a blueprint, He starts to draw line after line.

Have you ever watched someone drawing?

When they first start you, you think, "What is that supposed to be?"

There are lines all over the place. Slowly, line by line, the picture starts to come together. You see and understand things that you did not before.

An Entrepreneur

Since you have gone through the training that God takes apostles through, you become an entrepreneur.

You are put in a place where you learn to do new things. I am talking about a spiritual quality, not a natural quality. God takes you through experiences in life and training to change your character, so that you can become an entrepreneur.

However, you are not just becoming any entrepreneur. You are becoming God's entrepreneur.

We see many of them in the world, but if you see a true apostle, you will see one that never was an entrepreneur. This is someone who did not always make it. Yet, God took such a vessel, stripped them away, and then built and created in them a character to see what others do not see.

They will build what others could not possibly imagine. That is the role of the apostle. They are to lay a foundation for the Church. They are laying out a blueprint, the doctrine of the apostles that the other fivefold ministry can come and build on.

That foundation better be Christ and Him glorified. It better be Jesus alone and not your ideas, plans, thinking, and abilities. It better not be your skills, knowledge, and principles, because that is not an entrepreneur. That is just someone that studied well.

An apostolic entrepreneur is someone that can come up with something fresh that is God and God alone. That is the character that is forged in the apostle.

Understanding all Fivefold Ministries

Being that he has gone through all this, he starts to realize the importance of the other fivefold ministry. In order to get to be an apostle, you have to work through the other fivefold ministries as well.

People have this idea that the apostle is all on his own. No, there is a progression through the five. If you want to get to the office of apostle, you are working through the other four first, so I hope you took notes.

You may not stand in each office, but you will have at least touched on them. That is what qualifies you. How else are you going to work with them?

The apostle is meant to be bringing the team together. Unless you get what the team is doing and understand them, how can you call yourself an apostle?

It is like those guys in business that work themselves through the ranks. They make the best bosses. It is because they talk to you and know exactly where you are at.

They know what you are going through and they know what to expect from you because they have been there. They are the best team managers.

There is nothing worse than working for someone who was never in your shoes. They just got handed everything and think that they can just bark orders. They are not nice to be around because they do not get it. They did not work their way there.

Working Through the Ranks

It is the same in the church. An apostle is someone who thinks five steps ahead of everyone. They have been where you are, and lived, and gone through so many things. They end up becoming a trendsetter.

They do not even try to become trendsetters, but they just are.

When I look at Peter, I see a perfect example. We see him there at the crucifixion, talk about a stripping. He denied his own Lord. The worse was that Jesus knew he would do it.

Peter just about wanted to die. He was stripped of absolutely everything, his great boasts and his place as one of the twelve. He had nothing except that after all he went through, he still loved the Lord.

After all the stripping, he kept within him that little germ that God had planted there all along. It was upon that that Jesus said, "Ok, you are a stone. Upon this rock, I will build my church."

He was saying, "Peter, I know that you failed and messed up, but I am going to raise you up. I have been gearing you to be an entrepreneur. I have been gearing you, Peter, to start a movement."

Little did Peter know that not much longer after that, he would be visiting the house of Cornelius. He did not know that he would be opening a door that none of them could have imagined.

Even when they walked with Jesus, none of them could have imagined that they would reach the Gentiles. Although, if you look at the parables, you can see that Jesus was trying to tell them that all along.

Suddenly, the power of God came down on the Gentiles and everyone was taken by surprise.

"I guess the grace of God has been extended to the Gentiles."

Peter opened a door and set a new trend that we are most grateful for and are living and walking out today.

That is the role of the apostle, to open up these doors. He is the builder of the Church.

He brings solidarity in the Church. He brings authority and confidence. He also brings the entrepreneurial anointing. These are the character traits that God develops in the apostle through training.

FIVEFOLD MINISTRY – THREE ROADS

Chapter 07 – Fivefold Ministry – Three Roads

In the previous chapters I have painted a picture for you of what each of the fivefold ministry looks like. I have outlined some of their training and some of the character traits they will develop because of it.

The Three Roads: Ministry, Business and Social

Now the greatest mistake that we can make is to limit the Lord and our calling to the Church. We are called to be a light in the world and not just behind the four walls of the church building. Your calling should extend way beyond your ministry borders. If you can grasp that, you will see that your vision is bigger than you realize.

Because of the change that you have gone through in ministry, you have also been equipped to excel in both the business and social world.

Is it any surprise then, that we are seeing the Lord raise up leaders in both the marketplace and in social media who are changing the way that we view ministry? "Doing the work of the ministry" is no longer being defined as someone who stands behind the pulpit. It has extended to working on the streets, in the entertainment world or in the market place!

This is indeed a fivefold ministry for a new generation. One where the Lord Jesus is raising up His leaders in every social and economic realm. Where the name of Christ and a call to accountability is no longer limited to the church building, but being spread like wildfire throughout every social and cultural archetype.

As you have come to accept and embrace your call to one of the fivefold ministry, realize that the change this training has wrought in you does not end at the church doors. It has only just begun.

With this change, you are called to be an influence in every area of your life.

That is why you will often hear me talking about "the three roads." We are called to excel as Jesus did – crossing boundaries and reaching the entire world.

When you look at each of the character traits that are forged into these five ministries, the penny starts to drop as to why the Lord has you where you are. Remember what I said before how the character change that the Lord takes you through in ministry training is permanent?

Well that is what I am pointing out now in this chapter. There are too many who lead a double life. You walk out the changed character trait in your ministry, then revert back to the "old" you at home and work.

No more! The Lord changed you for a reason. Rest in that change and carry it through to every area of your life and you will see how you can use this training for ministry to help you succeed in both your relationships and your business life.

I am going to look again at the ministry traits of each of the fivefold, but for now, let us take a look at what each of the fivefold ministries look like in both the business and social realms of life.

The Evangelist on the Social Road

Let's look at the evangelist on the social road. What kind of person would he be there?

He is the kind of friend that is going to shake things up. If you come and spend time with us at one of our ministry centers, you will see each one of our team functioning in at least one of these.

If you are socializing or receiving ministry from us, you are going to receive ministry from all of the fivefold.

My passion is to watch, not in the ministry times, but in the social times. The evangelist has a way of putting his foot in his mouth.

He shakes things up and says, "That is not good enough. That is not God! Why don't you do it this way?"

They shake things up and they bring conviction without trying to bring conviction. They make people aware of their actions. However, the great thing about them is that they are ones that will always believe in you.

Being that they can see the right and wrong, sin and righteousness, they know the power of the Blood. No matter how useless and hopeless you are, there's always hope... as long as you do things God's way.

"I know that you are a mess. I understand. Yet, you must change and do things God's way!"

They will follow through and travail with you. They will always be there to point their finger. They make very passionate friends. You are never bored around people like this. You never know what to expect or what will come up.

Passionate Friends

You say, "Let's watch a movie."

The evangelist says, "No. The spirit on this movie is awful. I cannot do this."

They are fun because they never let you settle or just be complacent. We are always trying to push someone into a mold saying, "This is how you should be."

Using Your Ministry Character Traits

No, you should learn to walk in the anointing that God has given to you. Take the character traits that God has put in you through these years and apply them.

Are you an evangelist? If so, make things interesting. The next social gathering that you are at, open your mouth. Stir the pot and start a fight or something.

Does that sound too politically incorrect to you? I can tell you this, the deepest relationships in my life are the ones I had to work for! The ones I travailed through.

You are going to bring life and fire. It's only when you have a good fight that you become real friends with someone anyway. Shake it up a little bit.

Isn't that what life is about with relationships? Would you always like a friend that says, "Of course you don't look fat in that dress?"

An evangelist would say, "You look so fat in that dress!"

We need people like that.

Can't you see that this is the way that God has been gearing you?

Don't be afraid to open your mouth and say it like it is. Sometimes we need that. That is a real friend to me, someone that will say it straight.

However, there are also times when I need a friend that is going to sugarcoat it. We will get to the pastor soon enough.

Being an Anchor

All of us need those anchors in our lives that are not afraid to get in our face, say it straight, and put it out there. Then, you can really take a good hard look at yourself. If you have such a friend, you should count yourself very blessed.

They keep life very interesting.

The Evangelist on the Business Road

How can God use such a character trait in a business setting?

The evangelist is a risk taker. He is not afraid to make decisions. When they know that something is of God, they will step in there and do it. Then they will wonder, "Why isn't everyone else doing this as well?"

They are not afraid to jump in and say, "Let's do it!"

The leader will say, "I have this idea and plan."

The evangelist will say, "Let's do it and let's do it now. Let's give it all we've got! This is God. Let's go!"

They are passionate and fearless. Can you see that as God has developed these traits for you in ministry, you should be pushing them over into the rest of your life?

God has been preparing you to be complete all along. However, you are so singular in your purpose that you are incomplete.

The Pastor on the Social Road

Now, what about the pastor? He is the kind of friend that always follows through. He is the kind of person that always has the right advice at the right time. He is a good listener.

He is not going to judge you. In fact, he is the one that is going to say, "I understand."

Even my three-year-old knows who to go to for what. He knows the suckers. He knows those he can say, "Please please" to and then they will say, "I understand." He may be very difficult, but the pastor will understand.

No matter how full of rubbish and sin you are, they are the kind of friend that will listen and still understand you.

Sometimes you know that you need a smack and you know that you are wrong, but you need somebody to love you anyway.

"I know that I am in sin, I know that I am wrong. I know that I should die to my flesh, but I need five minutes to have my little moment here."

That is when you go to the pastor because the pastor will give you that five minutes. However, the evangelist will not.

The evangelist will say, "If you know what your sin is, why are you not dealing with it? Why are you not repenting right now? You know the truth! Don't whine to me if your life is falling apart. You know the truth."

I Understand!

Evangelists are great when you need that hard line. However, sometimes your heart is bleeding and you just need someone to say, "I understand" and that is all the conviction that you need.

If you are a pastor, it is so easy to do that in ministry. When someone comes to you, you can put your hand on their shoulder and say, "Hey, I care. I am there for you."

So, why are you finding this so hard to do on the social road? Why can you not do that with the people around you?

In ministry, you are the nice guy. You are always pouring out and there for everyone. Then, you go home and get into a fight because you have so many hard lines and you are so difficult to live with.

You are always trying to do things your way and you are pushing. Perhaps your natural character is coming out. Maybe you're a driver and you like perfection. Yet, in ministry, you would never guess.

Natural vs. Spiritual Character Traits

When you are in ministry mode, you pour out with all that training that God has given you and then you come home and you are a totally different person.

How about pulling some of that across? Why not take that pastoral heart that you show behind the pulpit or to your flock, and show it to your kids?

Why don't you show this heart to your spouse, friends, family, and those around you? Why are you not bringing that to the party?

You might find that there are more people gathering around you, just to be able to talk. That is what I love about someone who is pastoral. They just let you talk. They listen and understand.

They are not big talkers, jabbering your ear off, and calling down fire and brimstone. When the time comes, they will open their mouth and give you that word of advice and it will hit you straight between the eyes.

We all need that. If God has taken you along this road, you need to start walking in that anointing in this realm as well.

The Pastor on the Business Road

When the Lord starts using the pastor in business, you will see one who is a good organizer. He is going to be diligent and he is going to get the job done. As a pastor, in your training, you had to be a leader, follow through, and go through a lot of testing.

You were challenged and pushed beyond your limitations and you learned to become more than you were before. You learned to push through and excel. No one else was going to do it, so you were the buck. You were the one that had to do it.

If the meeting hall needed to be organized, the church needed to be painted, or there was an event that needed to be done, guess who was organizing everyone and everything?

The pastor is the one making sure that everything is done. Since the pastor had to go through that training, he was stretched so much. This is why, in the realm of business, they are very diligent.

They will always push through to the next level and follow through. They are nice to have around. They usually become the backbone of the business because they plod on no matter what.

Anointed Organization

They are loyal. They have stick-ability. In fact, that is the one who trains the new guy. If even the world can do these things, with natural traits, then how about doing it with the anointing?

That's really what should set us apart. I am not just talking about natural abilities, but ones that have been wrought through the fire. They have gone through that affliction and been embedded with the anointing of God.

How about taking what you have learned in the ministry and start using it in your business and social road?

You will start to see that everything that your hand touches will prosper.

The Word of God says that we will be above and not beneath, the head and not the tail. Everything that we touch will prosper. We will find favor everywhere we go.

How about taking what God has developed in us and stretch our hands out on these other two roads and find that favor and success in everything that we do?

You have your success to a limited degree in your ministry, but you have a double portion here. You do not just have the character traits that God has developed in you, but you also have the anointing in it.

You can use the anointing in your fellowship and business. God's favor can be upon it. You have the upper hand here. You can become that city on a hill.

However, for those that have been in ministry, if I say something about business, it seems like such a jump. If I say something about social environment and entertainment, this is also a huge jump.

No, it is not. Just take what you already have and carry it over. It is the same character traits and anointing, just a different environment.

This is how we are going to start seeing a church that is completely under God, in every area of their lives.

The Teacher on the Social Road

What about the teacher? He is a great problem solver. If you have a question, he has an answer.

The thing that I think makes the teacher the most fun in the social setting is that he is the best storyteller. He knows how to tell a story that is interesting. He is the one that can tell a good joke.

Storyteller Extraordinaire

He is someone who is fun to talk to and listen to. Also, he knows a little bit about everything because he knows how to learn and he has had so many experiences in life that he's had to work through.

He has stories that he can tell you from all over the place. He is fun to chat to and glean from. His general knowledge is amazing. So, in the social setting, it is so exciting.

However, if you are so spiritual and only used to doing that in the church, when you come to the social setting, instead of being fun and sharing those things, you sit down and shut up.

You're only deep when you stand up and teach. How about using some of that fun character that God has developed in you and using it in these other realms?

How about getting into the conversations and sharing illustrations, stories, and being entertaining? I like people like that. I like to hear things that I have not heard before. I like to be educated in a fun way like that.

I can always tell a teacher when it comes to a setting like that. When they talk, they say, "This reminds me of a situation where this happened and I heard this story. That applies exactly to this spiritual principle that we are living right now."

We may be busy talking about something or going through an experience, and a teacher will say, "Do you know what a good teaching this will make? This whole story makes such a good illustration for my next message."

That is the teacher for you. He always has a story and something to share. He has a head full of knowledge. However, unless you impart that knowledge, it is just knowledge and not wisdom.

Teachers are Fun!

You can be fun. It may be hard to imagine, but teachers can be a lot of fun. You would not think so, eh?

When you see a teacher, you see the guy at the chalkboard with the piles of notes and scriptures. Yet, that is not true. A true teacher is entertaining. They make you laugh. They tell you things that last with pictures that remain forever.

How about using some of that in the rest of your life, instead of just ministry?

You may even make a friend or two.

The Teacher on the Business Road

On the business road, it is even better. They are the best problem solvers. They know how to find answers.

That is why I love teachers.

"Teacher, this is wrong. Figure it out."

I just need to say, "This is the problem" and then I let him loose. He goes and finds the answer. It is awesome.

However, we keep limiting this to ministry. How about taking this and saying, "What is your financial or business problem?"

Find yourself a teacher. Say, "I need you to help me work through this. I need to do it God's way."

He will find you an answer. Scriptures will come to his mind, along with principles, things he has learned, and experiences that he has gone through. Even books that he has read will suddenly start to come up.

He will say, "Let's try this and this."

"Ok, that did not work. Let's try this."

"That did not work either. Let's try this."

Good Trainers

He will keep going until he eventually finds the answer. That is the nature of a teacher. They are fantastic in the business realm. They are the best troubleshooters.

He is also one that becomes a very good trainer. He says, "If this does not work, try that. If that does not work, try this."

"You are doing this all wrong. You are going to want to adjust this and that."

That is a teacher in the business realm.

Here you thought that you could not do business. You can!

If God has been pushing you there, He has been giving you the anointing and the ability to do it. You are just not using what He has given you. You are waiting for God to give you a whole different thing.

You were in ministry and now you are in business, so you think that you are going to get a whole bunch of new tools.

Why not just take the ones that you already have and then let Him add those new tools to you in that new realm?

He is not going to give you something so foreign to you that you have never touched before. He is going to take you from one place to another. Take your comfort zone with you.

It is so easy. You are already starting to look at your strengths and character traits and thinking about how you can use them in the social and business roads.

You are not tapping into the fullness of your potential.

The Prophet on the Social Road

Let's move onto the prophet. The prophet is the best motivator. He makes you feel positive about the road ahead. The prophet is fun to be around in the social setting. You can come there glum and leave smiling.

"Come on! Don't be so down. Let's go have some fun."

With a prophet, you can expect anything. Also, like with the evangelist, you can expect the naked truth. They will just be straight with you as well, but they have a better balance because they have a lot of compassion.

Ultimate Motivators

They are definitely motivators though. They give you a boost to your day. Could you imagine that looking at some prophets?

If you are a prophet, that is what you are capable of in a social setting.

When you stand up behind the pulpit, you are motivating the body of Christ. You say, "The body needs to come together. Jesus not only died for you, but He has given you the power to overcome every problem in your life.

You have the Holy Spirit inside of you. You can flow in the gifts of revelation. You have a place and you do not have to be downtrodden. Come on, rise up and touch God! Embrace Him!"

Why can't you do that on the social road?

You are so busy doing that behind the pulpit and thriving in ministry, but in a social setting you are so intense. You are too deep, sitting in the corner scowling at everyone. You cannot talk ministry, so what are you going to say?

Why not try being fun in the social road, as well as in ministry?

Come on, you can stand up and be the motivator in ministry, how about being passionate and motivating at the next barbecue that you have?

"Hey, you are looking great! I see that you did something with your hair."

Is that such a stretch for you?

You can identify the place and purpose of each person in the body of Christ. You look at them through God's eyes and you see their potential, as a prophet.

Why can't you do that when you step out of your ministry role?

When you step out of your ministry shoes and into your everyday shoes, why can't you continue being that person that sees the good in people? Why can you not see them through God's eyes, whether they love the Lord or not?

Why can't you see them through God's eyes and see something to love and motivate?

In ministry, it is easy. When you meet someone you say, "Lord, what do you want me to tell this person? I know that you probably want to motivate them and give them a word. You want to encourage them."

You are thinking to yourself all the time, "How can I encourage this person?"

That is how a prophet thinks in ministry, so why can you not think like this when you are not ministering?

Carrying It Over

When you are out with unbelievers, believers, family, friends, or even a school reunion, why can't you continue saying, "What can I say to bless this person? What can I do to motivate them and help them reach their potential?

What can I do so that by the time they are finished speaking with me they are ready to take on the world?"

Why can't you use that character trait that God developed in you, in ministry, and use it in your social road?

Yet, you have to wait until the anointing comes and then you stand up and are passionate and a blessing to the Church.

The blessing is not going to take place behind the pulpit. You sit in a church and receive for a few hours, but the real blessing comes in the day to day living out your calling with the people that are around you.

You are going to take snatches from the messages that you listen to and they will have an impact, but the real change comes when you walk it out.

When you can take what you do in the pulpit and invest it daily with everyone that God brings to you, you are going to see real change. The change is not going to happen behind the pulpit, but in your daily life. Take it with you.

The Prophet on the Business Road

When it comes to business, the prophet is also the motivator. They are the ones that motivate the team to action. When business is down and the finances are dead, they are the ones saying, "Let's do something about this."

They are also the ones that can get revelation, decree, release, and inspire. They are the ones that will knock on heavens doors and ask God to do something on behalf of the business.

They have everyone's backs because they are the motivators.

I really saw this in action when we got a very large order that we had to do in the past. We used to make all of our books in house. So, every one of our books were made by hand. This was quite a task.

It was a very large order that had to be completed in just a few days. Everybody had to get in there and do their thing.

You could see the prophets, "Come on guys, we can do it! Just one hundred more books today. Let's get going. You are doing a great job."

They were singing in tongues and praising.

Jessica was calling down fire! She went around laying her hands on every book.

"In Jesus name, whoever gets this one will feel the power of God!"

We had the evangelists calling down fire, the prophets motivating, and the teachers saying, "Ok, this did not work. What are we going to do to fix this? This piece of equipment just broke. We need to go and get a new one."

The troubleshooters were putting their heads together trying to figure it out.

The pastors were saying, "It's ok guys. Does anyone need a cup of tea? I will bring the tea. I am here for you."

"Are you struggling with your job? Let me help you. Let me support you in the best way that I can."

It was fantastic. I looked at that and thought, "Wow, the fivefold ministry in business action."

The Apostle on the Social Road

This now leaves the apostle. Being that the apostle is an entrepreneur, he brings everything together and creates an environment for good fellowship.

I used to have this crazy idea that good fellowship just happens.

Well... it doesn't!

Do not put a bunch of strangers in a room and think that they are going to have great fellowship. It does not work. People stare at each other and size one another up, especially us women.

Creating an Environment

You have to create an environment. You know what I mean. I am sure that you have gone to some parties before. There are some that are arranged very well, but others where everyone stands around not knowing what to do.

People are thinking, "Can I go home now? This is not comfortable or fun. Everyone is in their own clique."

If an apostle is involved in such a fellowship, they are bringing the groups together and bringing unity. They are creating an environment where things happen "naturally."

You will say, "It was so natural."

It really was not. The apostle just put it together.

Before we start our seminars, my husband usually stands up and says, "Guys, this is how everything is going to go. We are family here. You are a part of us now. Let's do this."

He creates an environment where you can let your hair down and begin to relax. When you start relaxing, then fellowship does happen naturally.

You will begin to chat with one another, exchange email addresses, and become friends. However, it initially takes someone to bring that together. It does not just "happen."

That is why we need apostles to not only be functioning on the pattern for their ministry, but to bring this pattern into every area of God's children's lives.

We need this balance. We need to learn how to get along with others and come into unity.

The Initiator

The apostle is also the initiator. He is the one that comes up with the ideas.

He says, "Hey guys, this is what we are going to do. I have come up with this idea. This is how we can do it."

Then, the rest of the team can jump in and do it.

He comes up with ideas that no one else has.

"Let's write our own songs and make our own songbook. I know that everyone else does it differently, but I am bored from being the same. Let's do it differently."

"Let's come up with our own way of doing meetings. How about we flow as God leads us?"

"Why not just set a new standard and create an environment where everyone is comfortable?"

It is fun. When you have someone like that in the social setting, it is not deep or heavy. This is why they make such good spiritual parents. They bring everyone together.

If God has called you to be an apostle, what does your social life look like? Are you the one coming up with the ideas for the next birthday party?

Why not?

Why aren't you coming up with ideas of how to bring everyone together? Why are you not coming up with a plan of how to break down walls?

This is one of the things that God challenged me on. I can do the apostolic thing, the teaching and ministry. I even have lots of books. Of course I can do that.

However, the Lord started dropping spiritual children at my door. Now, I could get along with all of them, but to get them to get along with one another was a whole different thing.

"Lord, I have a great relationship with each one. However, sometimes they are killing each other."

Breaking Down Barriers

I had to learn how to break down walls between them and get them to relate to each other.

The Lord said to me, "Colette, the importance of your ministry is not just your relationship with them. The defining mark for your ministry will be their relationship with one another.

You are not always going to be there. They need to be able to back one another, just like my disciples backed one another."

Jesus did it perfectly. After He left, His disciples continued in the doctrine and the pattern.

Why?

It is because He taught them how to be a team. He taught them how to flow together. They slept in the same place and ate the same food. They lived together.

It was not all ministry. They would go and minister to the masses and then Jesus would come back to the quiet place with His disciples. There He explained what He did one step at a time.

He created an environment. He pulled them out of their natural comfort zone and put them in the middle of nowhere. Then, He trained them how to get along with one another and fellowship together.

He did one amazing job because they were from all walks of life.

If He would have just left them to naturally get along with one another, there would have been bickering. In fact, there was some bickering with James and John coming and some asking about sitting at the right or left hand of Jesus.

They bickered and complained about things not being fair. That is still happening in the church today.

The apostle brings everything and everyone together. If God has called you to do that, are you bringing things together on the social road?

Are you arranging those social events to make sure that relationships are being developed?

It is not good enough for you to develop relationships with people. That is just the first step. You should be getting people to develop relationships with each other. Is that not what Peter and Paul spent all their time doing?

Bringing Unity

Did they not travel from church to church, getting unity amongst believers?

They had the guys at Jerusalem getting donations from the other Gentile churches because they were about to go through a famine.

You had this continual swapping and crossover. These things did not happen naturally. The apostles had to work hard at this.

Let's work a bit on this social road and create an environment. We need to live Christ every day. That is the role of the apostle on the social road. When it is done well, it is fun.

It took me a while to realize that this was as much my responsibility as standing up and preaching. Fortunately for me, the social road is my husband's forte. So, when I am having a day when I am not feeling very apostolic, I let him do it.

That's the great thing about having a spouse standing with you, side by side. You can do it together.

THE BUSINESS APOSTLE – A NEW BREED

Chapter 08 – The Business Apostle – a New Breed

What about the apostle on the business road?

I think this is very clear. Since the apostle is very entrepreneurial, he is always coming up with new ideas. He also has his finger on the pulse of everything that is going on around him.

He not only has the ability to start new things, but he also has the wisdom for it. God gives the apostle a vision and a plan, along with the anointing and ability to follow it through.

He has an ability to make and train. If you can do it in ministry, you can also do it in business.

However, do not think that you can do this the other way around. Don't think that just because you are successful in business that you are going to be successful in ministry.

You have to start with the temple like Solomon did, then you can work your way to the other two roads. You have to get the anointing first. Otherwise, you are just going to do things the world's way.

You are going to end up getting into the flesh. You will do business the world's way, dog eat dog. You will be the big head honcho, pushing everyone else down. You are going to think you are doing it God's way, but you are just using natural personality power.

If God has been pressing you to let go of business and get more into ministry, it's not because He is trying to strip you. He just wants you to do it His way.

Doing It God's Way

If you feel that God has a business calling for you, but He seems to be taking it away from you, it is because He is saying, "Too much of what you have is the world. I want to give you something fresh and new."

He is removing you from that and putting you back into the ministry, so that you can have your character formed according to His pattern. Then, you can receive the anointing to displace the spirit of the world that is in you.

Then, He will lead you back into business and you will be able to flow and get ideas and wisdom. This time, however, you will do it with His hindsight and His eyes. You will flow in His anointing and everything that you touch will prosper.

Your business will be a vessel that He can use for your ministry.

Don't think, "I don't feel like touching ministry. I am just going to do business. Therefore, I can bless the ministry."

No, you are just appeasing your guilt. You are not doing it God's way. You are doing it the world's way.

Just because you are good at business, it does not mean that God has called you to do business. He can raise up any monkey to do that. Anyone can do business. The world is doing it all the time.

His Character - His Power

What sets us apart as believers is that we do things with His character, power, and anointing. It is actually a shortcut. If you got that, you would dump the business so fast.

Sure, it will take a bit of time to get into that season of letting go, having your mind renewed, and receiving God's pattern and vision. Yet, when you go back, it will be like getting into the front seat of a Ferrari and putting your foot down.

When you do business this way, it will be a tool that God can use. It will be something that God has done and not something that you have created with your own hands.

If you say, "I built this business from the ground up," then do not tell me that you have been called of God to do it.

You just said that you did it yourself. What do you need God for?

Don't do what you find so natural and then baptize it with the Word of God. That is not what I am talking about. I am talking about doing business with God's power and character. I am talking about doing it with what He has established in you.

Then, we can be a Church that is a city on a hill, separate from the world. This means that you are also unlimited in what you can accomplish.

When God Calls you to Business

If you are doing it the world's way, then that is all you have and know. However, it turns out that we serve the one that created this world. He has seen and knows the loopholes that you cannot begin to imagine.

He has a vision and plan, beyond your expectations. The problem is that your mind is so limited and it has been shaped by the way that the world functions. All you see is the impossibility.

"I cannot start my own business because of this, this, and this."

Who said so? God?

No, that is the world's voice. They have programmed the way that you think.

God knocks at your door asking you to let the business go.

"God, you called me to business. Did you not?"

Yes, He did. That is why you have to give it up. Before you can flow in business God's way, you need to build the temple, like Solomon.

You cannot be a Solomon just because you are good in business. Solomon built the temple first. It is because he built the temple so well that he succeeded in everything else that he put his hands to.

If he would have just done the business side, I wonder to myself if he would have accomplished everything that he did.

He did not just build one road. He started by building the temple and because of that, he moved onto building palaces. He even built entire cities.

Go and look through the Scriptures and you will see that there is a whole list of cities and towns that Solomon built.

He built an aqueduct, started trade routes, and built ships. He expanded into so many areas that no king or judge before him had ever done. Actually, no king after him came close to what he did either.

All this was because Solomon started with the temple. Start building the temple and dedicate your life to the Lord. Ask him to break you down, shape you, give you a pattern, and let you see like He sees.

When you go back into the world, you will see in black and white. You will see the world's way and God's way. That has to set us apart.

I am weary of seeing businessman in the world that look like the world saying, "I am making lots of money. Therefore, I am blessed."

Then the richest man in the world must be a born again believer and an apostle, if that is the guideline that you are using.

Is Money a Guideline for Success?

Are you using money as a guideline for success?

If that is the case, then Bill Gates must be a pillar of the church.

Money and success in the world is not our standard.

Success and favor is obvious for us because we are blood-bought. However, we should be doing it with His anointing and power.

Don't think that just because you are doing business God's way and you are evangelizing that now you are a business apostle.

That just makes you a believer doing business, who also evangelizes.

Don't call it a calling. It is just a job and that is all that it is. I know that this may be a hard word to receive, but it is about time that everything came in line.

It starts with the Lord and with the Spirit.

Becoming a Builder

I promise that if you build that temple, what started out as just an idea or pattern will be covered with gold.

For Solomon, it did not stop there. It continued into the palace, the ship yard, the trade routes, and the cities. Solomon gave Hiram a bunch of towns. Hiram said that they were a piece of junk.

Solomon developed them. He saw potential in them that Hiram didn't.

Hiram is a clear picture of doing business the world's way. He took a look at these cities and said, "What are you doing this to me for, brother? These are a bunch of junk."

Solomon thought, "Obviously, you don't see with the eyes of God - the eyes of wisdom."

He showed him the difference between the way that he did business, and the way that Hiram did business. Solomon rebuilt those towns and made them flourish.

> **What the world sees as an opportunity for failure, God sees as an opportunity for success.**

God sees with different eyes. You see above your circumstances and through the problems. Yet, you cannot have both. There is a progression. You must start with the temple and work your way through.

Then you will find success, not in just one area of your life, but in all three areas of your life.

Of course, it is a price to pay at the beginning. However, when it is all said and done, you will say, "By His grace."

You will know that it is God that built it. Solomon knew that it was God. Read through the Proverbs, and again and again you will see him saying, "God established me. Just obey the wisdom. If you are wise, you will follow after God and obey His commands."

"He made me the king that I am and gave me everything that I have."

Every other king out there was boasting about the deals they closed and the cities and towns that they took. Solomon, who did even more, said, "It is God that did all of these things."

That is the point of it all, isn't it?

Bringing the Three Roads Together

At the end of the day, it should be God that brings all of these roads together. Those characteristics that have been shaped within you, are from the Lord. Don't be afraid to use them.

However, if all the characteristics that you walk in were shaped by the world, you need some reshaping. Perhaps this will explain some of the upheaval that you are going through.

You have been coming to the Lord saying, "Use me."

Yet, you are so comfortable on these other roads that a tug of war begins. You do not understand what's going on.

"Why is there all this discomfort in my life?"

God is trying to say, "These character traits here, you got from the world. You were indoctrinated with the spirit of the world. They taught you to do it that way.

"Your heart and desires, I put there. That was the germ thought, since you were a child. There is nothing wrong with that desire. However, you have learned to walk it out the world's way.

"You need to let that go and allow me to reshape your character, according to my pattern. When I shape your character this way, it will be infused with power and the anointing. It will change you into something."

David's Character Shaping

David knew that kind of shaping. As he was going through his trials, running from Saul, how many times did he fall on his face before the Lord? The Lord saved him again and again.

He did not do anything without asking God first. It shaped his character.

Then, we look at Saul. He did it the world's way, didn't he?

He stepped out there, a king, looking for the big and the strong. No one is singing about Saul today. He is more like the shame of Israel, not the hero of Israel.

However, David was a hero.

Why?

Saul's character was shaped by war and by the way that the kings of his day ruled. David's character was shaped by the Lord and the circumstances that he had to go through.

He sought God again and again. Each time he did this, God added something to him. God changed him, until he became a mighty king.

Let God shape your character. When He does it, you will always be destined for success because His Word tells us that If we need anything, we just need to come to Him and He will give it. (Matt 21:22)

Nothing is impossible for Him. We are meant to be a success and walk in favor. We are meant to be above and not beneath, best in the city and country, in business, ministry, and social.

We are meant to be blessed. There is only one condition. We need to do it God's way and with the character that He has developed in us.

If we can do that, we are set to start a new generation of the fivefold ministry. It will not only be in the church, but a generation that this world will see and recognize as something fresh and new.

It will shine brightly and burn strongly. It will not be all talk, but it will carry the power to bring real change.

THE FIVEFOLD MINISTRY PURPOSE

Chapter 09 – The Fivefold Ministry Purpose

Ephesians 4:11-13

> *And He Himself gave some to be apostles, some prophets, some evangelists, and some pastors and teachers,*
> *12 for the equipping of the saints for the work of ministry, for the edifying of the body of Christ,*
> *13 till we all come to the unity of the faith and of the knowledge of the Son of God, to a perfect man, to the measure of the stature of the fullness of Christ*

Amongst so much talk about what the fivefold ministry is and what they look like, there comes a time when we have to brush all of that aside and ask ourselves, "What is their core purpose?" While each will express their calling in a way that is unique to that office, we must not lose sight of why we have these offices in the first place.

In a church age when so many clamor for a title of recognition, we quickly lose the core purpose of why the Lord put that calling on us in the first place. So let's get back to brass tacks shall we?

Now that I have explained why we have the fivefold ministry and what they look like, how about we look at their purpose in the Church?

There is no better explanation than the one we find in Ephesians 4! Paul went into great detail on what the fivefold ministry was meant to be doing. He might not have outlined their individual functions, but in this passage it is quite clear that he wanted us to grasp why they were set in place.

I have broken the passage down for you, so that you will never forget why you are given the title you hold.

Regardless of your ministry title, vision or call, there are six purposes that we should all be completing. So when you look at your ministry, can you go through each of these points and say with conviction, "I am fulfilling the purpose for my call"?

By the time you finish these last few chapters, you will answer that question with a confidence that you never had before.

1. For the Equipping of the Saints

As my mind wanders to the fivefold ministry I see a Bride in her chambers being prepared for her wedding day. I see her servants fussing around her, fixing her hair and making sure that every wrinkle is smoothed out of her dress.

This is the task that the fivefold ministry is meant to be performing. How can the bride of Christ walk down the aisle all disheveled? We are called to equip and prepare her for the big day!

It is no surprise that the Church is facing a level of spiritual warfare as it has never seen before. Well the fivefold ministry is what will equip the Bride for that battle. They are called to smooth out her dress, put a sword in her hand and equip her for the task ahead.

Sometimes we get so hung up on taking the land and establishing this new move that is upon us, that we forget that the Church needs to be ready for this battle. Who will equip the Church and make sure that she is armed and shielded for this new phase of warfare?

It is for the fivefold ministry leaders to take up the task. We need to assume our position as a gift to the Church and to be the servants we are called to be. So many consider the call to the fivefold an elevation, but I am here to remind you that it is a call to servanthood.

This is a call to serve the Lord and to serve the Church. To equip her for the steps she needs to take. Is the Church in a place where she can hear the voice of God for herself? Is she able to follow the orders of her God? Is she presentable to Him? The question is rhetorical and in that we see how much work we still have to do!

The Gifts of the Spirit

It stands to reason that to accomplish this equipping, that you will need to flow in the gifts of the spirit. You will need to function in prophecy and the gift of faith (to just mention two) to equip the Church. Here you begin to realize that the gifts of the Spirit are simply tools that help you to do your job.

They do not define your job – but rather assist you in this high call to change the Church and in so doing, to change the world.

2. For the Work of Ministry

There is something to be said about a housewife that works day in and day out to take care of her family. It is not a job title that is written in lights, but for the family that comes home to a warm meal, it is worth its weight in gold.

The day to day running of the house of God is what we call the work of the ministry. Yes, there are times that you will be called to stand behind the pulpit to edify or equip, but it is the work of the ministry that will bring about the most change in the Church.

It is the hours you spend ministering inner healing or helping someone break free of demonic bondage that establishes your call. In an age of titles, so many make the mistake of thinking that all of that "dirty work" should be left to the pastors, while the rest of the fivefold flits about town, making a name for themselves.

So What Do You Do Exactly?

I met someone who was sharing how she had started a prophetic school. Having been on this road for many years myself now, she had a few questions and mentioned how she makes sure that the prophets that come to her for training do not "flip out" but are stable and emotionally constant. I smiled thinking to myself, "Boy, has she got a few things to learn about real prophets!"

I challenged her a bit on doing the work of the ministry. I said,

"Yes, a mature prophet needs to stop swinging the pendulum, but if you are going to run a school, it is for you to help them work through the hurts of the past and the oppression that pushes them into that emotional havoc. You cannot just demand that they have it together, if you did not take them through the things that cause them to fly off the handle!"

She responded with, "Oh when hurts and emotional outbursts come up, then we just send them to Christian counseling. When demons manifest, we just send them to a team who does deliverance."

All the while I am thinking to myself, "So what exactly do you do in this prophetic school of yours?!"

So she does not take them through dealing with triggers from past hurts. She does not follow through with removing the influence of demons to help them get set free. The bottom line? She stands up front every week and tells them how to prophesy and then teaches them to flow in the gifts of the spirit – everything that is "fun" about prophetic ministry.

Colette Toach

The Central Pillar

What about the other purposes? I would daresay that the work of the ministry is the central pillar on which the other purposes hang!

You cannot "outsource" problems and hard work, just because you do not like to get your hands dirty!

It is not just for the pastors to follow through and travail long with people. Regardless of your fivefold calling, you are called to the work of the ministry!

You are called to counsel, pray, deliver, equip, arm, instruct and so forth. If you want to know what kind of ministry you should be doing, read Romans 12:6-15 and discover that there are in fact 12 different aspects to doing the work of the ministry! If you are not performing all of these, then you are not fulfilling your purpose in the Church.

The Diversity of Anointing

Now the way that an evangelist will teach, deliver and serve will be very different to the way that a pastor does it. We get a bit caught up on ministry types just like that prophetic school teacher did.

"Send people with demons to the evangelists."

"Send people with hurts to a pastor."

Our difference does not lie in our service or even the gifts of the Spirit, but they lie in the anointing through which those gifts are manifest in our lives!

Would it surprise you to know that some of the greatest deliverance ministers are teachers and not evangelists? Because the evangelist functions so strongly in the external anointing, demons manifest more during their ministry.

However, to deal with a demon, you do not need to be an evangelist! A teacher is well able to pick up the sword of the Word and bring deliverance as well. He will just do it differently and with a different anointing.

Have you been seeking the Lord about walking in greater authority or for help on dealing with hurts of the past? Have you been desiring to cast out demons and be equipped to preach? You do not need to change your calling to do that! You simply need to identify the anointing that you function in and then do the work of the ministry in that context!

You do not need to become a prophet to prophesy. You do not need to become a teacher to teach. While these are tools that these ministry offices tend to lean towards, they are just that... tools! You are well able to function in all of them with the anointing you already have. Simply embrace your uniqueness and realize that the way you bring deliverance or even how you deliver a prophetic word will differ, depending on your ministry office.

3. For the Edifying of the body of Christ

Who do you go to when you have a bad day? Is it hard to imagine that the Lord has called you to give people the strength to continue on with their walk?

I cannot tell you how often the Lord has used Craig and I to simply give someone the motivation to press on. We see so many that seem to make a shipwreck of their calling (as Paul calls it.) We sometimes are tempted to think, "Ah they just gave up! They do not have the conviction to press through. They allowed the devil to win that war."

Has it occurred to you, that sometimes the war rages so loudly in the mind of a believer that it drowns out the voice of God? Yes, it does not mean that they should fall prey to the voice of the devil, but what voices are there competing with his voice?

Do the voices they are hearing sound like,

"If you do this, you will lose everything."

"You know that if you walk away from this now, you are making a mistake."

"You know if you go down this path, you are headed for destruction."

Doesn't that all sound like good advice? Yes, the kind of advice that adds rhythm to the voice of the enemy who continues to tempt them to give up the fight until they relent by saying, "I do not care! So yes, I am going to let God down. Yes, I am going to fail, but right now, I do not care. Let me just fail!"

Fivefold Ministry Edification

It is in moments like these that we need a word that edifies. That competes with this raging war inside of us!

That is when we need an evangelist to say, "God is able to keep you! The Holy Spirit is holding His hand out to you right now –take it!"

We need the pastor to say, "I understand this struggle inside of you – you need a break. Let's see what we can do to help you see things from a new perspective…"

We need the teacher to say, "Your mind is so full of accusation of the enemy – did you know that this is just a spirit of guilt and condemnation and you can bind it in Jesus name? Come let us bind these attacks so that you can see clearly again…"

It is for the prophet to say, "I can see that right now you are in a storm, but the Lord wants you to know that there is peace in the storm and if you will take His hand right now, there is a whole new field of blessing that is waiting for you!"

It is for the apostle to say, "I know that you feel this attack is unique to you, but everyone the Lord calls faces it. Let's see what we can learn from this so that you can rise above it and use it to help others break free as well! The Lord did not lead you this far for nothing!"

Now that is what edification looks like. When we are at our lowest point, no matter which fivefold ministry we run into, that meeting should end with edification and the power we need to run another race.

4. Till We all Come to the Unity of the Faith

Take a look at the Greek for the word "faith" in this context:

4102 pistis {pis'-tis}

AV - faith 239, assurance 1, believe + 1537 1, belief 1, them that believe 1, fidelity 1; 244

1) conviction of the truth of anything, belief; in the NT of a conviction or belief respecting man's relationship to God and divine things, generally with the included idea of trust and holy fervor born of faith and joined with it

1d) belief with the predominate idea of trust (or confidence) whether in God or in Christ, springing from faith in the same

I want you to recognize that the word faith here is not referring to doctrine. It is not saying that we have to bring unity of doctrine to fulfill our purpose. If you make that your goal, then you have a long way to go. You will be on a journey that will never end. Even Jesus had a hard time with this amongst His disciples!

He knew why He came to this earth, but their doctrine said He was to become a mighty leader that would overthrow the Romans. He had just a small group to work with and bringing their doctrine into unity was a challenge, so you are not doing too bad!

Fortunately for us though, this passage is telling us that we are required to bring the Church to a place of conviction in their faith in Christ. Faith is always based on a person. You cannot have faith in... faith! You base your faith on what a person says or does.

Our faith is based on Jesus and His Word and this is exactly the kind of faith that you should be establishing in the hearts of God's people. To teach and instruct, to bring each one to a place of true conviction of who they are in Christ.

Now again, each ministry will do that differently! The teacher will bring conviction through the Word. The prophet will bring conviction by revealing the heart of Jesus, and the evangelist will bring conviction through the agency of the Holy Spirit!

Imagine then how well-rounded the Church would be if all of the fivefold just did their job? Imagine a believer who is brought to conviction through all of the fivefold ministry! There is not a single part of their lives that would remain untouched. They would become a complete man - equipped to do good works of every kind!

5. And of the Knowledge of the Son of God

This purpose follows on so beautifully from the previous one! Once someone's faith has been established in the Lord, it is time to come to a true knowledge of Him.

These two purposes intertwine! The more you come to know the Lord, the stronger your conviction becomes. The stronger your conviction, the more you come to know the Lord!

Doesn't it seem strange to you though that Paul would slap this little line in here? He is talking to the Church here at Ephesus. These are not new converts. They are mature believers, yet he says to them how the fivefold needs to bring them to a knowledge of the Son of God!

Do not be so surprised – the Church today is not terribly different. There are so many who love and serve the Lord, yet do not truly know Him in an intimate way. It would be as if they are a bride in an arranged marriage that follows protocol, but does not really know her husband intimately.

This is why you are called to reveal the complex character of the Lord Jesus to the Bride. The Lord sure knew what He was doing when He set the fivefold in place for this.

Because of the unique character and relationship that each of the fivefold have with Him, they are equipped to share this aspect of His nature with the Church.

If you have walked a while in the Lord, you come to realize that the nature of the Lord is full of complexity and color.

I have been married to my husband since 1995 and I would daresay that I know him pretty well.

However, as we mature and life plays out, I discover yet more sides to his character I never knew before. When he became a father, I saw a side of him I never had before. When he took my daughter for her first driving lesson, I saw a side I never had before.

When our first child started dating, I saw a side of him I never had before! The more we walk through life, the more our character is developed and shown for the world to see. Now if a human being has so much complexity, then how much more, the Son of God?

The Diversity of Character

You have come to know the Lord Jesus in your own set of circumstances. You know Him in the way you worship Him and how you receive from Him. However just change your circumstance or enter into a new season of your life and you will find that His nature is far more reaching than you first realized.

I have walked with the Lord all my life and I have to come to know His nature as the Father. I have come to know His nature through the Word and His nature as the Son. His nature as the Spirit is passionate! However, no matter how many times He shows me different aspects of Himself, He continues to surprise me!

Now each of the fivefold ministry has a very unique relationship with the Lord. They know Him in a very specific way. A way that imparts to them the anointing they have. They know Him in a way that gives them the outlook they need to fulfill their call.

So when you get all of them together, what will you find? You will find a full picture of what the Son of God is truly like! Each ministry reflecting the nature of the Lord in a different way – together forming a beautiful picture of perfection!

Fivefold Ministry Reflecting Christ

The evangelist portrays for us the fiery nature of God! He portrays His passion for the lost and His hatred of the enemy! He reminds us that ours is a God of action – a consuming fire!

The pastor portrays the mothering nature of God. The nature of one who nurtures and protects, without fear for His own life. This is the nature that took Jesus to the cross to pay for our sins, so that we would not have to.

The teacher portrays the mind of Christ to us. He shows us the side of God that challenges us to know more and to walk in greater wisdom. To understand and to do and not to be swayed by compromise! To stand firmly in a foundation of both knowledge and wisdom – having our minds transformed!

The prophet portrays the passionate Groom to us. The lover of our souls that woos us into the secret place and whispers His adoration for us, reminding us that we are His and He is ours.

The apostle portrays the authoritative nature of God, reminding us that we serve a righteous Father that although we fear Him, we can also run to Him, wrap our arms around His neck and say, "Abba father!"

If we could but take a piece from the nature and experience of God that each of the fivefold has, we would know God in His entirety. Yes, there is always a deeper intimacy and knowledge to be had in the Lord. I do not suppose that I would ever be able to say in this lifetime, "I know everything I need to about the nature of the Lord. I know every part of His character."

It is because just when I come to fall in love with one part of His nature, He shows me how much more there is to Him. This makes for a passionate love affair with the Lord. It is this passion that the fivefold ministry is meant to be kindling in the hearts of God's people.

If only they could all come to a knowledge of God – then their faith would be on a firm foundation!

Colette Toach

6. To a Perfect Man (To the Measure of the Stature of the Fullness of Christ)

This word "perfect" does not mean to be without fault. Rather, it means to be an adult. To be mature. To grow up! How many in the Church have never left the phase of "rebellious teenager"? They continue to be swept around by every wind of doctrine.

Flitting from revival to revival to get a fresh touch from God, because their personal spiritual life went stale. How many are still trying to find out who they are?

When I was in high school, the guidance counselor drilled me about what career choice I wanted to follow. I had no idea back then what I really wanted to become. I had some desires and careers that would fit my interests, but I could not really say that I "knew" what I wanted to become when I left school. I just had a few directions, without a clear purpose. It took me some time to simply grow up.

It took time for me to settle down and not want to just "party" and have fun. It took me getting a job, getting married and having a few kids to make me see with mature eyes.

It is the same in the Church today. We have a body full of members who do not know what their place is. They are either still in "party" mode or they have simply given up on trying to find their place and are wandering from here to there, chewing on whatever tastes good!

It is your job to tell the Church in no uncertain terms to, "Grow up!" It is time for you to help them find their place and to bring them to a mature walk in the Lord.

I think about how much Paul struggled with that when he wrote to his churches. The Galatians should have grown up, but in many ways they ended up going backwards to childhood again! He tells the Corinthian church that they should be eating meat by now, but that they are still sipping on milk! He tells them that they need to grow up!

So how do each of the fivefold cause the Church to grow up?

Well the evangelist is the one with message just like Paul had,

> *1 Corinthians 3:3 You are still worldly. For since there is jealousy and quarreling among you, are you not worldly? Are you not acting like mere men? (NIV)*

That was a wake-up call to make God's people see their immaturity, inspiring them to grow up and to become like men!

The pastor is the one who will take the church and give them a model of maturity and prepare them for success. Just like a parent would raise up a child to become independent and successful, so also is it the pastor who will give the Church the tools that it needs to take the world by storm!

The teacher? Well that one is clear! Coming with the meat, his call is to bring the church to maturity through the Word and doctrine. To wean them from the breast and move them onto eating a T-bone steak!

The prophet brings maturity by helping each one see what their purpose and place is in the body of Christ. While he also brings them into a relationship directly with God, his causes the Church to "grow up" by making each one aware of their call and responsibility in the Body! They are the ones that give believers their "first job." There is nothing quite like working for the first time to make you grow up, and in this spiritual context, it accomplishes the same thing!

The apostle brings it together and puts each one in place and trains them to fulfill it. He watches over each one and does not afford them the luxury of complacency. He is a policeman in many ways, pushing the Church to excellence, and does not allow complacency to set in – dragging them back to infancy!

The Journey Begins

The purpose of the fivefold ministry is but the beginning of what the Lord has for the Church. It is for us to equip and prepare her, but that is not the completion of what we are meant to do. Once she is equipped, then the good works can begin!

Only when she is armed, can she begin to take the land. So there is always a higher place to go to. I have spoken in this book (and for the rest of the series) about the fivefold ministry for today. I have outlined who they are and the task that is before us right now.

However once our job is done, I daresay the journey just begins for the Church. For it is then that we will see her take the promised land and we will see the walls of Jericho come down. It is here that we will need these leaders once again to send out the battle cry and lead the way into the fray.

There is no lack of teaching in the Church about what God has promised us. Whether your teaching is on the end times, or if it is on bringing the Bride into maturity – we need to stop and ask ourselves, "How will we bring this to pass?"

How will we make the Bride without spot or wrinkle? How will we prepare the Church for the coming of Christ? How will we aid the Church in entering their Promised Land? The answer is the same, regardless of what vision you have for the future. We need leaders to enable the Church to fulfill its God designed destiny.

God has given us the revelation. The Word has given us the pattern. The Holy Spirit has anointed, and the Father has appointed. Jesus has shared with us, His heart. What are we going to do with all of that? Sit around and wait for the Lord to do it all by Himself?

No, since the beginning of time, God always worked with man and He is asking to work with us once again. To usher in a New Move. To set His perfect plan into place. All we need to do is our part. We just need to build, establish and make sure that the blueprint is followed. Then we can trust the Lord to bring the fire.

I am going to end with two visions that I have shared in other places - so if I am repeating myself, just roll with it!

A Vision of the Mighty Warriors

Many years ago as I sought the Lord about my place in the Church, He took me high above the earth and as I looked down, I saw the earth as a chess board. One by one, I saw the Father place the chess pieces on the board. Each piece was made of solid gold.

Then as He put the last piece in place, suddenly the entire board ignited into a raging flame. The Lord told me that these were His mighty warriors. He explained that He was at work, pulling them out of obscurity and setting them in place and when the last one is set, that we would see a revival spread throughout the world.

The revival would not be limited to just one nation, church or denomination. Rather, we would see Him move across the globe simultaneously. As the years have progressed, I have seen the Lord do just as He promised.

He has raised up His mighty warriors - men and women, spanning the board of the fivefold ministry, suddenly finding their place. At the time I had this vision, the prophetic was just coming into its own and the apostolic a hushed whisper in the Church. I look around now and see a momentum that is not ending any time soon.

A City on the Hill

The second vision that the Lord gave me, came when I was seeking him about my apostolic call and the future He had for His church. In the spirit I was standing in an open field and looking towards the sky.

As I looked on, I saw pieces of a building, made of gold, beginning to drop from the sky, as if placed on the ground by an unseen hand.

One by one, the pieces came down, it started to form a temple. From there construction continued until a city was built – one that shone for miles around. The Lord shared how He was giving His apostles the pieces of His pattern for His Church. That the picture would not come all at once, but that He would give it a piece at a time.

The goal though was clear – to build His end times Church until it became a city that is set on the hill. Make no mistake, the Lord has a clear blueprint for His Church. One that is laid on the foundation of Christ and operates in the power of the Spirit, according to the mandate of the Father.

The question you need to ask yourself is, "Where is my part to play?"

Are you allowing the Holy Spirit to cement you into place? Are you willing to allow Him to lift you up from your place of comfort, and be thrust into this new move? This book has only just begun to scratch the surface of what His mighty warriors look like.

As you continue in the series, each one will become more defined and a clearer picture will start to come together. I highly recommend you read this series alongside *Called to the Ministry* where I teach about how your call is progressive.

Find your place child of God. See where the Lord is putting you right now and fulfill your purpose with everything He has put into you. Together we are going to set the world on fire.

THE LOCAL VS. UNIVERSAL CHURCH

Bonus Chapter – The Local vs. Universal Church

In the books to follow this series, there are a couple of terms that I use all the time that need a bit of explanation. These two terms are: The local and universal Church.

This chapter has been taken out of a teaching on the pattern for the Church, and it is not directly part of the teaching on the fivefold ministry. However, I felt including it was necessary if you want to continue working through the series.

The Early Church

When the early Church began, we find Jesus traveling with His disciples from place to place. We do not see something that was set in stone. Yes, there were some places that they visited frequently, but there was no "single place" where they met for every single gathering.

The gathering at one specific place only came about after the Day of Pentecost when the Holy Spirit came and Peter stood up to preach and three thousand were saved in one day. What do you do with three thousand people?

The rebirth of so many believers meant that a whole bunch of cells were just added to the Body! Where are you going to put them all? Some order needed to be established and so the apostles rose up and started putting that order together.

What was the best thing for them to do? They started to send them to people's homes.

Do you know how incredible it is when a conception of a child takes place? From day to day the size of that embryo doubles.

Well, that is what happened here in the Church. They just started with their little group. They started with twelve and then they had 120 gathered on the Day of Pentecost. Suddenly there were cells springing up all over the place.

From that moment onwards you hear about believers meeting at rivers and in homes, but it still was not good enough. You had a heart over here, lungs over there, and a leg moving around here.

It was chaotic and it took the apostles to bring it all together.

Seeing as though it was all happening at Jerusalem at that time, they set up their headquarters over there. From there, as the apostles took their place, all those churches and members were able to take their place and function as they were meant to function.

Do you read about Peter saying we have three thousand people, so now we need to build a building?

He does not say, "Oh this Sunday meeting is going to be so great because I have three thousand people to preach to."

He does not ramble on about being the head apostle and therefore he is the senior pastor with all the other people being under him, being assistant pastors. He does not get everyone together to start a building fund.

The Local Church Personality

No. Let us just read the book of Acts and stick to the Word here. That is not what Peter and the other disciples were called to do. They were called to connect the body parts.

They did not jump in there and say that meetings were being held at Apostle Peter's house on Monday, Apostle John's on Tuesday and so on. No! They had 120 people that could do that job.

Those 120 knew the teachings and they knew Jesus. They had Timothy, Silas, Agabus and many other people named that were not the big apostles. What we are looking at here are leaders that functioned within the local church.

And so they took those three thousand and got together with them.

Now when you are such a big group and you invite people to come to your house, I think it would be natural that certain kinds of people would connect with certain kinds of people.

You must keep in mind that Jesus had only done His ministry actively for three years. So, though that small group had known each other for a while, you would not say that they were a solid family that had been together for years and years.

Members Connect With Each Other According to Interest

Therefore, they are more than likely going to connect on common interests. They are going to connect by what burns in them and I daresay that you would find these members of common interest coming together like magnets.

Certain ones would be drawn to one another. I am sure that as they came together, that you could see that one group started looking like a "heart" and another like a set of "lungs". What I love about this picture is that each one is unique.

1. Each Local Church is Unique

The greatest revelation that the Lord has given me since He started to teach me about the local Church is that each small group of believers that come together is unique. That is one of the main things that has gone wrong in the Church today.

We are trying to make sausages. We just want to squeeze them out and have them all look the same. There is a reason why the Word of God speaks of us as a bride and a body.

Where have you ever seen two people that are exactly alike all the way down to their fingerprints? Then why in the body of Christ should it be any different when we are referred to as members?

Even when it comes down to our organs and features, every single one of us is unique. So, when it comes to the local Church, what we are talking about here is a small group of people that have gathered together with the same vision, heart and love for the Lord.

I think that the biggest mistake we can make is to try to squeeze them into what we think the mold should be. We should not say that all churches should have bible studies every week.

In this case, all the prophets would think to themselves, "Kill me now!" Each one is unique. We look at 1 Corinthians 16:19 and it says,

> *The churches of Asia greet you. Aquila and Priscilla greet you heartily in the Lord, with the church that is in their house.*

That is how they did it in the book of Acts. They got together in one another's homes and it was so practical. There was a church in their house. It does not say a bible study group. It says there was a church in their house.

Why is that? It is because a church is two or three gathered together in His name.

2. Gathering According to Common Interest

They each started getting together in the houses and they each started developing their own personalities. They had their own flare and likes and dislikes. Nonetheless, in these little groups, things started happening.

They were little churches in a community. Each one of them looked different. They all had the same Spirit and the same Lord, but each one was different.

Just look at a group of people as a whole. Some people just want to go soul winning, some have a burden for the elderly, and some just really have a heart for the poor. The Lord has given us such a variety right here in the midst of us.

3. The Local Church is Where People Live

The local Church is where people live. Every one of us faces daily challenges and stress. The local Church is where people should have access to come to every day. The Word says that, "The church was added to on Sundays..."

Well, it does not say that in my bible. In my bible it says that, "The church was added to daily." How did that happen? It happened because the Church was a living, breathing organism. Every single one of those local churches were so alive, on fire and full of power that there was no way you could not be attracted to them.

All you needed was one of those in a community and it was like a light where the moths would gather. And so the Church grew and multiplied.

When a married couple had a fight, they had their local church to go to and receive counsel and prayer. If people were having a hard time at work or experiencing persecution they joined together and prayed.

When Saul was persecuting the Church, the believers got together and prayed for Saul in love and the Lord came to Him leaving him flat on his face before God.

4. The Local Church is Like a Family

The local Church is where people live and things happen practically. This is where you are going to see the gifts and the ministries manifest. It is where everyone will have a hymn, song or a word.

> *1 Corinthians 14:26 How is it then, brethren? Whenever you come together, each of you has a psalm, has a teaching, has a tongue, has a revelation, has an interpretation. Let all things be done for edification.*

Everything should be alive and ongoing. It is not just something that happens once a week. It should be a home. This is why having a home church is so beneficial. However, I am a bit reticent to call it a "home church" because you see church in a home when I say that.

You see a place where you have your praise and worship, prayer, bible study and then you go home. That is not what the home church that I am speaking about is. Rather it should be more like a family home.

If I could think of another word for "home church" that is what I would choose. We should go and start some families. Let us birth some babies and start some families.

Isn't that what Peter did? He birthed three thousand and then the next thing you know there were families being formed all over the place.

There were connected believers that loved one another so much that if someone did not have a chair they would say, "Take one of ours." These people sold their goods and gave up all they had.

Who do you do that for in the natural? Saved or unsaved, you do it for the ones that you love. You do it for your family, don't you? If your son, daughter, mother or father does not have something, then you do not hesitate to find a way to help them out.

You will sell things to help them out. That is how the Church was in the book of Acts. They were a family.

The Universal Church Personality

Now just as the local Church is a collection of cells in one place, the universal Church also has some clear characteristics.

House and Temple

Firstly, it is a place where large gatherings take place. Here you will find a variety of callings, passions, and interests. Where the local Church usually centers around a specific purpose, these public meetings will reach every kind of believer with every kind of passion.

It says in Acts 2:46 that they continued daily with one mind in the temple and they broke bread from house to house and ate their food with gladness.

They had these two aspects. They had the breaking of bread from house to house, and they had the temple where they all met from all the local churches. You have your family church and you have the universal Church where believers from every walk of life gather.

One is public and one is personal.

1. Public Meetings

The function of the universal Church includes public meetings, preaching and getting the leaders together to tell them what they should be doing and teaching to God's people.

From there leaders can go and filter it down to their local churches.

2. Being Sent Out

Functioning in the universal Church involves being sent out. In each instance the apostles were sent out to reach unchartered territory.

In cases where there are lots of believers, like in Samaria, apostles were sent to go and lay hands on them so that they could receive the Holy Spirit and then get the organization set up and everything put into place.

3. To Establish Structure

The apostles did not stay there though. Apostle Paul told Timothy and Titus to go and appoint elders in every city. He did not tell them to go and play church. He told them to appoint elders and get the members together.

Working with the universal Church means helping local churches find structure and discovering what kind of organ they are in the Body. Once again, depending on the kind of fivefold minister you are, how you will accomplish this will differ.

4. Distribution

It says in Acts that everyone came and laid everything at the apostles' feet. They gave all the finances to the apostles at each headquarter and from there it was distributed to those that had need. Working in the universal Church involves distributing between members so that everyone is blessed.

This relates to financial and spiritual things!

Apostolic Function

It is so simple. However, what would happen if you factored the apostle out? This is what the Church has done. You have churches, sure, and they are all members and each one has their little hobbyhorse and that is good.

The Lord told me that each one is meant to have their hobbyhorse. That is the fire and the vision that the Lord has given them. This is why you go to certain churches and all the pastor seems to preach is this one thing over and over.

However, that is the member that he is and those are the members that he will draw to himself. We should stop knocking that, because that is their call and their vision. The apostle should be encouraging that so that they can find their place in the body of Christ and fulfill their function because not everyone can fulfill the same function.

If you are not happy about what they do at that church, then find another church that you do like. However, do not try and change them, because the fire that they have has been placed in them from the Lord.

Colette Toach

Having "Hobby Horses" Makes us Unique

You should know that no one can take away the fire that God has placed in you. We are meant to be varied and have hobbyhorses. This is what makes us unique. We cannot all do the same thing.

How boring would it be to have a family of kids who all looked identical, had the same personalities and all answered questions in the exact same way? I am an expressive. I would be bored out of my mind. I need variety, drama, and stress in my life to make it interesting. I thrive on it.

It makes life worth living. Let us start doing something real in the body of Christ! As you continue through the series, I will help point out our differences and the power of finding your place.

From here, move on to *Today's Evangelist* and allow the Holy Spirit to begin putting the picture together for you.

About the Author

Born in Bulawayo, Zimbabwe and raised in South Africa, Colette had a zeal to serve the Lord from a young age. Coming from a long line of Christian leaders and having grown up as a pastor's kid she is no stranger to the realities of ministry. Despite having to endure many hardships such as her parent's divorce, rejection, and poverty, she continues to follow after the Lord passionately. Overcoming these obstacles early in her life has built a foundation of compassion and desire to help others gain victory in their lives.

Since then, the Lord has led Colette, with her husband Craig Toach, to establish *Apostolic Movement International,* a ministry to train and minister to Christian leaders all over the world, where they share all the wisdom that the Lord has given them through each and every time they chose to walk through the refining fire in their personal lives, as well as in ministry.

In addition, Colette is a fantastic cook, an amazing mom to not only her 4 natural children, but to her numerous spiritual children all over the world. Colette is also a renowned author, mentor, trainer and a woman that has great taste in shoes! The scripture to "be all things to all men" definitely applies here, and the Lord keeps adding to that list of things each and every day.

How does she do it all? Experience through every book and teaching the life of an apostle firsthand, and get the insight into how the call of God can make every aspect of your life an incredible adventure.

Read more at www.colette-toach.com

Connect with Colette Toach on Facebook!
www.facebook.com/ColetteToach

Check Colette out on Amazon.com at:
www.amazon.com/author/colettetoach

Recommendations by the Author

Note: All reference of AMI refers to Apostolic Movement International.

If you enjoyed this book, I know you will also love the following books and recommendations.

Today's Evangelist

Book 2 of the Fivefold Office Series

By Colette Toach

As an evangelist, you are called to start churches, to bring life to the dead, to bring people into the embrace of the Holy Spirit, and open their eyes to the power of Christ. You are a fire starter. You were never meant to sit at home waiting around for the Lord. No, rather you are called by the Lord to go out and to bring His wildfire to the nations so that He may consume the darkness and enlighten the people lost and wandering around in the dark.

Now, if you are going to start a wildfire, you need to know where you come from, where you are going, and how you will get there. You need to understand the power that you hold and how to wield it.

In this book, Colette will show you where the evangelist came from, what their role is in the fivefold ministry, and how and where they operate. So be prepared to go higher and understand your call as an evangelist like never before.

Called to the Ministry

By Colette Toach

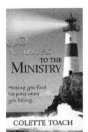

God has put a purpose for your existence inside you. There is a driving force within you to accomplish something much greater than yourself and to fulfill the call of God on your life. However... how do you know what that calling is?

Apostle Colette Toach takes you by the hand and helps you to realize the call of God that has been whispering to you all along.

How to Hear the Voice of God (Study Group Kit)

By Colette Toach

Knowing the Lord is more than just understanding the principles of the Word. It is learning to know when He is speaking and to share in the secrets in His heart.

By the time you are finished with this course, you will discover that God does not have favorites, but that every believer can hear from Him clearly.

If you are ready to experience the reality of the Lord in your life, then dive in!

Fivefold Ministry School

www.fivefold-school.com

You Can Be a Success in Ministry!

My passion is to see you realize yours! I understand the years in the desert. I know what it feels like to have a fire shut up in your bones, knowing that God has something greater for you.

That is why together with my husband Craig Toach, we have trained up our own Fivefold Ministry team and in association with apostles all over the world, we hold in our hands the resources to launch you into your ministry!

Here is What We Offer to Prepare You for Your Fivefold Ministry Calling

- Identify Your Fivefold Ministry Calling
- Disciple and Mentor Relationship
- Ministry Certification, Credentials and Ordination
- Ministry Training Materials That Are Totally Unique
- Fivefold Ministry Training That Affects More Than Your Mind
- Student Only Benefits

Colette Toach

Contact Information

To check out our wide selection of materials, go to:
www.ami-bookshop.com

Do you have any questions about any products?

Contact us at: +1 (760) 466 - 7679
(9am to 5pm California Time, Weekdays Only)

E-mail Address: admin@ami-bookshop.com

Postal Address:

> A.M.I
> 5663 Balboa Ave #416
> San Diego, CA 92111, USA

Facebook Page:
http://www.facebook.com/ApostolicMovementInternational

YouTube Page:
https://www.youtube.com/c/ApostolicMovementInternational

Twitter Page: https://twitter.com/apmoveint

Amazon.com Page: www.amazon.com/author/colettetoach

AMI Bookshop – It's not Just Knowledge, It's **Living Knowledge**